Those
Tremendous
Mountains

Also by David Freeman Hawke

Those
Tremendous
Mountains

David Freeman Hawke

THE STORY OF THE
LEWIS AND CLARK EXPEDITION

W · W · NORTON & COMPANY
NEW YORK   LONDON

Printed in the United States of America

All Rights Reserved

First published as a Norton paperback 1985

Designed by Earl Tidwell

Library of Congress Cataloging in Publication Data
Hawke, David Freeman.
Those tremendous mountains.
Includes excerpts from the journals of Lewis and
Clark, first published in 1904–5 under title:
Original journals of the Lewis and Clark expedition,
1804–1806.
Includes bibliographical references and index.
1. Lewis and Clark Expedition. 2. Lewis,
Meriwether, 1774–1809. 3. Clark, William, 1770–
1838. 4. The West—Description and travel—To—
1848. 5. Rocky Mountain region—Description and
travel. I. Lewis, Meriwether, 1774–1809. Original
journals of the Lewis and Clark expedition, 1804–
1806. Selections. 1980. II. Title.
F592.7.H29   1980   917.8′04′2   79–18167

W.W. Norton & Company, Inc.
500 Fifth Avenue, New York, N.Y. 10110
W.W. Norton & Company, Ltd.
10 Coptic Street, London WC1A 1PU

ISBN 0-393-30289-X

6 7 8 9 0

*This book is dedicated to three friends
who helped make it possible:*

VERNON CARSTENSEN
WILLIAM DECKER
DONALD JACKSON

Contents

x   *Contents*

List of Illustrations

Author's Note
on the Journals

Here at the start it should be noted that the men's words and their grammar have been scrupulously respected in all quotations from the journals of the Lewis and Clark expedition, but their spelling, capitalization, and punctuation have been made to conform to modern usage. Thus, when one of the crew writes of a day on the Missouri, "We crouded Sail and Sail ᵈ 16 miles," his entry here appears as "We crowded sail and sailed sixteen miles."

Something has been lost in doing this. The grizzly bear becomes a more formidable beast when Clark describes it, as he is allowed to do in chapter 11, as "a verry large and turrible animal." Both Lewis and Clark spelled words as they pronounced them, and thus one can almost hear them speaking upon reading "fortiegued" for "fatigued," "norstrals" for "nostrils," "debth" for "depth," "wartered" for "watered." But a literal transcription of the journals' text has drawbacks. It can get in the way of the narrative. A reader can sometimes become so fascinated with the "ingenious phonetic atrocities," Clark's especially, as to ignore what the men are saying. Also, to a degree, it demeans them, making them seem less intelligent and informed than they were. Lewis, whose spelling was only a slight improvement on Clark's, might write "seen" for "scene" and "years" for "ears," but he could also spell and use correctly an uncommon word like "caparisoned." The journal entries were made at the end of long, often wretched and exhausting days. They were private records that both Lewis and Clark expected to polish before allowing others to read them.

Five journals of the expedition survive—three by members of the crew in addition to those of Lewis and Clark. Not a day of the more than two years spent in the wilderness goes unreported by someone. And yet for the historian, who always wants to know more, this copious recording lacks much. We are now aware, since the discovery of Clark's "rough journal," that at least Clark edited himself in what was long thought to be his original journal. On 1 August 1804, for example, he wrote in the rough journal: "This being my birthday I ordered a saddle of fat venison, an elk fleece, and a beaver tail to be cooked, and a dessert of cherries, grapes, plums, raspberries, currants, and grapes of a superior quality." Out went that personal note in the second draft. In another passage of the rough journal, written just after the barge—fifty-five feet long, manned by twenty-two oars—had nearly capsized, he remarked that it was saved only "by some extraordinary exertions of our party—ever ready to encounter all fatigues for the promotion of the enterprise." Out, too, went that praise for the men when he copied the entry into the notebook Thomas Jefferson would see. The President wanted journals of the Voyage of Discovery, as he called it. He did not want diaries.

Fortunately, Lewis was less restrained in his journal entries than were Clark and the men. He was livelier, fuller, and more personal. Days which Clark gave in a brief paragraph or two Lewis recounted in short essays that sometimes ran to two or three thousand words. His reports were precise and vivid. He wrote well. Often he caught a scene nicely in a few words. Once, sitting in the midst of a Nez Perce encampment, he remarked that "the noise of their women pounding roots reminds me of a nail factory." Another time, when the party hovered close to starvation, two men who were sent out to barter for food with the Indians returned with three bushels of edible roots. They had made, said Lewis, "a successful voyage, not much less pleasing to us than the return of a good cargo to an East India merchant." He did not hesitate to interject his private feelings, as on the day the party first sighted what they thought were the Rocky Mountains. "While I viewed those mountains," he wrote, "I felt a secret pleasure in finding myself so near the head of the heretofore conceived boundless Missouri. But when I reflected on the difficulties which this snowy barrier would most probably throw in my way to the Pacific, and the sufferings and hardships of myself and party in them, it in some measure counterbalanced the joy I had felt in the first moments in which I gazed on them. But as I have always held it a crime to anticipate evils, I will believe it a good comfortable road until I am compelled to believe differently. . . ."

What a modern reader misses most in the journals, even Lewis', is the absence of comment about the men. Only occasionally does an individual emerge from the group. By the end of the voyage, we know that Silas Goodrich excelled at fishing and Joseph Whitehouse at tailoring buckskin clothing, that William Werner and Thomas Howard were "neither of them . . . very good woodsmen," that Hugh Hall could not swim. But we know little more than that about them. The reader learns that all but seven of the crew were addicted to chewing or smoking tobacco but who the seven puritans were goes unmentioned. The single personal description of any in the crew comes from Clark about his slave York—a large man, "fat and unaccustomed to walk as fast as I." Someone once threw sand in York's eyes and nearly blinded him, but other than that incident the record gives no hint how the men felt about him. Moses Reed is a cypher mentioned only once, when he confessed he had "deserted and stoled a public rifle, shot pouch, and ball." Early in the trip John Collins was charged with "getting drunk on his post this morning out of whisky put under his charge as a sentinel." After receiving a hundred lashes for the offense, he blends back into the crew for the rest of the journey. We know that Pierre Cruzatte, the single man the captains called by his first name, which they converted into "Peter," brought along a fiddle which he played with abandon evenings around the campfire, but we know none of the tunes he played. Except for François

Rivet, who had a talent for dancing on his hands, the journals rarely mention by name the eight *engagés* hired for the first leg of the voyage. Oddly, the reader learns more about Scannon, Lewis' Newfoundland dog, than about the men. His yelps and howls as he treads on barbs of the prickly pear and writhes amidst swarms of mosquitoes are scattered throughout the journals.

The journals reflect the fact that this was a military expedition. Orders were issued and obeyed. Infractions were handled by court-martials. The men shaved regularly. (Once when traveling with a band of beardless Indians, Lewis and the men with him found it easy to disguise themselves as members of the tribe—"my over shirt being of the Indian form, my hair dishevelled, and skin well browned with the sun, I wanted no further addition to make me a complete Indian in appearance.") Yet the journals make clear that Lewis and Clark ran the expedition on a loose rein. They had an instinctive sense when to go easy and issue an extra dram of whisky or lengthen the nooning hour after a hard morning on the river. When among Indians, they did not deprive the men of social or physical intercourse with the "tawny damsels," but only asked that they not let fraternization undercut friendly relations with the tribes. And when the men came down with venereal disease, as several did, the captains did not moralize or tut-tut; they treated the disease as a matter of fact.

Doubtless there were fights and quarrels among the men that the captains passed over in the sanitized journals. A party of some thirty men cannot live two years in continuous harmony. Clearly, however, no dissension ever occurred between Lewis and Clark. To an army man a split command was a contradiction in terms. Leadership under combat conditions, which the expedition endured from start to finish, could not be divided. Final decisions must be left to the man at the top. Yet the split command of the Voyage of Discovery worked perfectly. It is only one more remarkable aspect of the most remarkable expedition in American history.

Part One

Preparations

Chapter 1

The Dream

The dream possessed Thomas Jefferson from youth. He grew up in Albemarle County, Virginia, where the Blue Ridge Mountains, an immense curtain that hid secrets from a curious boy, blocked the view to the west. Vague tales drifted in during his boyhood about the land that lay behind that looming wall—tales of treeless and seemingly endless plains, of a gigantic river called the Mississippi that rolled from Canada down to the Gulf of Mexico, and of another river called the Missouri that stretched maybe a thousand miles or more westward to a chain of mountains. Once across those mountains—no great feat if they resembled the Blue Ridge—a man might glide down to the Pacific Ocean if another river like the Missouri sprang from their western slopes.

Others besides Jefferson dreamt that Virginians would one day explore that mysterious country and eventually settle it. Virginia, after all, owned most of the vast territory. Its charter from the British crown granted it all the land between its northern and southern boundaries from sea to sea. When Jefferson years later said, "our confederacy must be viewed as the nest from which all America, North and South, is to be peopled," he only echoed on a grander scale a vision of his father, who talked often of penetrating the mysteries of that shadowy region west of the mountains; and of his teacher Reverend James Maury, who wanted an exploring party "sent in search of that river Missouri, if that be the right name of it, in order to discover whether it had any communication with the Pacific Ocean."

The Spanish and French knew much about that region but kept what they knew to themselves. Only after Great Britain acquired Canada from the French in 1763 did facts begin to supplant myths in the British archives. Occasionally an American contributed something that fleshed out the murky picture. Jonathan Carver of Massachusetts journeyed westward in 1766 and wintered with the Sioux on the Upper Missouri. Twelve years later he published *Travels in the Interior Parts of North America*, a book Jefferson read with care. Carver gathered from the Indians that the western mountain chain was much like the Appalachian system in the east, a single line of pyramid-like peaks that stretched from somewhere in Canada to the Gulf of California. The Indians called them Shining Mountains because, so Carver understood, they were coated with an "infinite number of crystal stones of an amazing size," and when the sun shone upon them they sparkled "so as to be seen at a very great distance."

In 1778, the year Carver published his book, Captain James Cook made a landfall off the Pacific Northwest coast, and for the first time the world knew the width of the North American continent. Cook had with him John Ledyard of Connecticut, another colony whose charter had let it claim a strip of land the width of its borders from sea to sea. Although the charter's authority had died with Jefferson's Declaration of Independence, Ledyard assumed he trod American soil when he stepped on the Pacific shore. "I felt myself plainly affected. . . . It soothed a homesick heart and rendered me tolerably happy."

Thomas Jefferson, painting by Charles Willson Peale
INDEPENDENCE NATIONAL HISTORICAL PARK COLLECTION

Jefferson feared Cook's discovery would prod the British into expanding their western claims into a region he dreamed Americans would one day settle. "I find they have subscribed a very large sum of money in England for exploring the country from the Mississippi to California," he wrote in 1783 to George Rogers Clark, the legendary Indian fighter. "They pretend it is only to promote knowledge. I am afraid they have thoughts of colonizing into that quarter." Would Clark consider leading an American party into that territory? Clark would, if Congress authorized and subsidized the venture. He did not think it would be especially difficult. "Three or four young men well qualified for the task might perhaps complete your wishes at a very trifling expense." Congress, overwhelmed with debts accumulated during the Revolution, gave no thought to the project.

Two years later Jefferson was in France as America's ambassador. While there he bought every book he could find that would help dispel the mysteries of the Far West. He met John Ledyard, then seeking to raise money to establish a trading post on the Pacific coast. When that project failed, Jefferson proposed to him to "go by land to Kamchatka, cross in some of the Russian vessels to Nootka Sound, fall down into the latitude of the Missouri, and penetrate to and thro' that to the U.S." Although Ledyard "eagerly seized the idea," he got only as far as eastern Siberia when Russian officials, suspicious that he might divert the fur trade from posts in Alaska to American merchants, aborted the trip and sent Ledyard back to Europe.

As President Washington's secretary of state, Jefferson may have had a hand in initiating the proposal made in 1789 that the army explore the Far West. After a year of desultory study the army concluded that it was "a business much easier planned than executed . . . [and] neither prudent nor practical [to trespass] with the sanction of public authority" on territory held by a foreign power. That same year Spain encouraged American emigration into the Louisiana Territory. "I wish a hundred thousand of our inhabitants would accept the invitation," Jefferson said. "It will be the means of delivering to us peaceably what may otherwise cost us a war."

In 1792 Robert Gray, an American, discovered what Cook had missed when he touched the northwest coast—an immense river pouring in from the east. He named it the Columbia, after the ship he captained. The size of the river encouraged hope of an all-water route to the Pacific, interrupted only by an easy portage over the Shining Mountains. The following year André Michaux, a French botanist, told Jefferson he wanted to explore the western country. He had made botanical excursions through much of the South and parts of Canada. Jefferson wrote a prospectus to encourage contributions to Michaux's project and drew up a set of instructions to guide him. The chief purpose of the exploration should be "to find the shortest and most convenient route to communication between the U.S. and the Pacific Ocean, within the temperate latitudes, and to learn such particulars as can be obtained of the country through which it passes, its productions, inhabitants, and other interesting circumstances." Jefferson made the trip sound like a jaunt. Michaux had only to travel up the Missouri River and "then pursue such of the largest streams of that river as shall lead by the shortest way and the lowest latitudes to the Pacific Ocean." The Shining Mountains were not an obstacle worth mentioning.

Nothing tangible came of Michaux's proposal, for he was soon enticed into a hopeless intrigue to invade the Louisiana Territory, then owned by Spain, with a force subsidized by France. But during the negotiations Jefferson got to know one of his neighbors in Albemarle County, a young man named Meriwether Lewis, then nineteen. The Lewis family was prominent in the county and Jefferson knew it well, but Meriwether Lewis could at best have been a casual acquaintance. Only later, when digging out facts to write Lewis' obituary, did he learn that the father had died when Lewis was four, that his mother had remarried and the family had moved to Georgia, that at the age of thirteen she had sent him back to Albemarle County to be educated, and that after two years of schooling he had turned to work the land inherited from his

Meriwether Lewis, painting by Charles Willson Peale
INDEPENDENCE NATIONAL HISTORICAL PARK COLLECTION

father. He also learned that young Lewis was "early remarkable for intrepidity, liberality, and hardihood, at eight years of age going alone with his dogs at midnight in the depth of winter, hunting, wading creeks when the banks were covered with ice and snow. He might be tracked through the snow to his traps by the blood which trickled from his bare feet."

Jefferson knew little of this when the young farmer approached him in 1793 and asked to accompany Michaux on his western travels. Lewis was not physically impressive—other than to remark that he was bow-legged, contemporaries had little to say about his appearance—but something about him impressed Jefferson, for eight years later as the newly elected President he asked Lewis to serve as his private secretary. In the years since the collapse of Michaux's proposal, Lewis had joined the army and risen to the rank of captain. His assignments had carried him throughout the Northwest Territory. "In selecting a private secretary," Jefferson told him, "I have thought it would be advantageous to take one who, possessing a knowledge of the western country, of the army and its situation, might sometimes aid us with informations of interest which we may not otherwise possess." The Indians who held lands bordering the eastern banks of the Mississippi especially concerned the President. Settlers were pushing into the territory, but the Indians refused to sell their holdings. Jefferson wanted to lure them from their ancient culture and semi-nomadic habits into the white civilization as peaceful farmers. Lewis could advise him how to proceed with this delicate project.

Jefferson told Lewis he would be one of the family, and so he became. He dined regularly with the President on meals cooked by a French chef and drank wines from a superb cellar. He lived at Monticello when Jefferson went there to escape Washington's torrid summers. His duties were not those of the usual secretary, for Jefferson handled all his own correspondence. Rather, he was the President's confidante. Also, Jefferson seems to have regarded him as someone to be molded for an important assignment, although exactly what was unclear when he brought him into the executive

mansion. Something like a father-son relationship developed between Jefferson, who was sixty and had no son of his own, and
Lewis, who was twenty-six and had no clear memory of his own
father. Consciously or not, Lewis soon adopted some of his men-
tor's idiosyncracies, such as writing "knoledge" for "knowledge,"
"it's" for the possessive "its," and beginning sentences with a small
letter.

In May 1801, a month after Lewis reached Washington, the
President learned of a disturbing rumor—Spain planned to cede
the Louisiana Territory back to France. Jefferson rested easy with
the land in Spain's hands. She cared little about it, had done nothing to develop it or to repress the French and British intruders who
tapped its rich source of furs. She was "too feeble" to hold it per-
manently and her encouragement of American settlers would in
time let the United States "gain it from them piece by piece." But
in the hands of France, led by the aggressive Napoleon, all would
change. An army of occupation and colonization by French citizens
would block American encroachment and create tensions that
could lead to war.

In airing these thoughts Jefferson began to transform Captain
Lewis, U.S.A., into a geopolitician. The rumor of retrocession
probably started both men thinking about an expedition up the
Missouri before the French took over, for "it is certain that on
their arrival they will instantly set on foot enterprises of a similar
nature." But while the idea gestated, another event, this one literary, brought it to fruition. Toward the end of 1801, Alexander
Mackenzie, a Scotsman, published a two-volume account of
his journey in 1793 across Canada to the Pacific Ocean. In his
final pages Mackenzie called for a program designed to block
American encroachment in the Far West. If an all-water route to
the Pacific existed, they must not have it. The Canadian border,
he said, rightly belonged somewhere around the forty-fifth parallel,
which would give Britain access to the headwaters of the Mississippi and in the Pacific Northwest bring the rich Columbia Valley
under her rule. American trading vessels that now regularly plied

along the northwest coast must be driven out. If Britain erected a line of forts across the continent, "*the entire command of the fur trade of North America might be obtained,* except that portion of it which the Russians have in the Pacific. To this may be added the fishing of both seas and the markets of the four quarters of the globe."

Mackenzie gave Jefferson and Lewis a moral imperative for launching an exploration of the Far West before the British, whom both despised, clamped a claim on it. He then did more by making such an undertaking seem a reasonable venture. He described himself as a man like Lewis, at ease in the wilderness, barely exposed to a formal education but "endowed by Nature with an inquisitive mind and enterprising spirit; possessing also a constitution and frame of body equal to the most arduous undertakings." Surely, what a Scotsman could do an American could do better. Mackenzie also wiped away what many had thought insuperable obstacles to such an exploration. The Indians had turned out to be friendly all the way out and back. The Rocky Mountains, as he called them, had at first sight presented a stunning view—an apparently endless chain stretching from north to south of snow-covered peaks whose tops "were lost in the clouds." But a river carried him to their base, and there Indians guided his party along "a beaten path leading over a low ridge of land eight hundred and seventeen paces in length." The seemingly impenetrable barrier had been crossed by a hard but, given the stupendous size of the mountains, relatively short portage. And on the opposite side he found another river flowing westward toward the Pacific.

Mackenzie's detailed chronicle—he listed the stores and provisions taken along, the amount and kinds of Indian presents carried, what the crew ate, how they packed their baggage—gave Lewis a handbook to use in the early stages of planning his own expedition. Mackenzie had traveled with ten men; Lewis planned to take "ten or twelve men" with him. Mackenzie taught himself celestial navigation before departing. "Capt. Lewis," Jefferson remarked soon after he had asked Congress to subsidize the Voyage of Discovery, "has been for some time qualifying himself for taking observations of longitude and latitude to fix the geographical points of the line he will pass over. . . ." Mackenzie took along a dog on his journey. Lewis, as if to deviate from the pattern would court trouble, planned also to take along a dog on *his* expedition.

Chapter 2

The Message

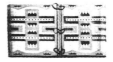

Jefferson officially initiated the Voyage of Discovery in a secret message to Congress dated 18 January 1803. In it he revealed himself as a deft and bold politician. He dared to ask Congress to join in a number of subterfuges to get his cherished expedition underway.

Spain presented the first problem. Despite the rumors of retrocession she still owned, as far as he knew, the vast Louisiana Territory through which the mysterious Missouri twisted. Jefferson pretended that Spain's lease would not obstruct an American exploration. "The field of knowledge," he said, "is the common property of all mankind, and any discoveries we can make in it will be for the benefit . . . of every other nation, as well as our own." Yet a month and a half before the message to Congress he had asked the Spanish ambassador whether his country would "take it badly" if the United States sent a party of travelers up the Missouri? The purpose would be solely for "the advancement of geography." The ambassador replied that "an expedition of this nature could not fail to give umbrage to our government." Jefferson did not advertise this rebuff. When asked by the French ambassador if Spain would grant permission for an exploration of its lands, Jefferson answered, "she ought to," and said no more. He was equally evasive in the message to Congress. "The nation claiming the territory, regarding this as a literary pursuit which it is in the habit of permitting within its dominions, would not be disposed to view it with jealousy, even if the expiring state of its interest there did not render it a matter of indifference." Why, then, the label *confidential* at the head of his message? Any alert congressman could see that Spain had not given permission to travel through its territory and that to vote for Jefferson's expedition would commit the United States to a trespass on the land of a foreign nation.

Having called it a "literary pursuit," Jefferson now asked Congress in his message to ignore the remark. For years he had held that the Constitution must be strictly interpreted. Nothing in that document, as he read it, permitted the government to back voyages of discovery. It did, however, allow for measures that encouraged foreign commerce. And so in his message he asked that the bill appropriating money for the expedition contain the words "for the purpose of extending the external commerce of the U.S." Thus, "the principal object" would fall "within the constitutional powers and care of Congress." Such phrasing, he added cryptically, "would cover the undertaking from notice, and prevent the obstructions which interested individuals might otherwise previously prepare in its way." He left it to Congress to determine or imagine who the interested individuals were.

Jefferson asked for a mere $2,500 to send his ten or twelve men on a journey expected to last at least a year and a half and to cover some six to eight thousand miles round-trip. The figure seemed ridiculously low, even after Congress had been assured that all members of the party would be military men "taken from our posts, where they may be spared without inconvenience." The

President did not make clear to Congress that the War Department would supply more than personnel. When Meriwether Lewis worked up an estimate for the voyage, he listed only $81 for weapons and $255 for camp equipage, knowing that the federal arsenal at Harper's Ferry would supply the bulk of arms; the army, the camp equipment. The only large outlays Lewis foresaw were the items that the army could not provide—river boats ($430) and Indian presents ($696). The final cost of the expedition, never revealed to the public, hovered somewhere between $40,000 and $60,000, depending on who did the accounting, or from fifteen to twenty times what Congress had appropriated.

The secret message leaked, of course, almost at once to the knowing in Washington. The Spanish ambassador thought the project would not proceed. He said, "the good judgment of the Senate does not see the advantages that the President proposes in this expedition, and that, on the contrary, they feared it might offend one of the European nations." The ambassador underestimated Jefferson's hold over Congress. Rarely did he propose a project before feeling out opinion at his weekly dinners for select members of the House and Senate, and rarely did Congress fail to give what he asked for. On 28 February 1803, Congress with little fuss approved the Voyage of Discovery and appropriated for it the sum requested by the President.

Chapter 3

Make Ready

Jefferson never doubted that Lewis—"brave, prudent, habituated to the woods, and familiar with Indian manners and character"—was the man to head the Voyage of Discovery. It did not perturb him that Lewis lacked a formal education, for he possessed "a great mass of accurate observation on all the subjects of nature which present themselves here, and will therefore readily select only those in his new route which shall be new." He had a quick mind combined with a remarkably perceptive eye that missed nothing that passed before him, and he had the further talent of being able to put down on paper precisely what he had seen. He was at once flexible and firm, able to swing easily from a bivouac in the forest to a drawing room in the President's mansion yet remain himself in both settings. He performed with painstaking thoroughness whatever he undertook. Some of these qualities—plus a fastidiousness unexpected from one happy in the wilderness—emerge in a blistering letter Lewis wrote about his tailor:

Of all the damned pieces of work, my coat exceeds. It would take up three sheets of paper, written in shorthand, to point out its deficiencies or, I may even say, deformities. . . . The lace is deficient. I had it taken to pieces and altered and could I have done without it, I should have returned it, beyond a doubt. For the blind button holes on the cuff he substituted lace and no part of those on the facing was worked blind. The four small buttons on the cape are deficient.

No doubt the tailor soon supplied the deficient buttons. A friend noted that Lewis "was always remarkable for perserverence." In the boy, this "seemed nothing more than obstinacy in pursuing the trifles that employ that age." In the man, one called it "great steadiness of purpose, self-possession, and undaunted courage."

Lewis and Jefferson began to make ready for the expedition weeks before the secret message to Congress. The crew would be recruited among volunteers drawn from western army posts. A flat-bottomed wooden boat large enough to carry a dozen men and three or four tons of baggage would be built in Nashville, Tennessee. After Congress authorized the Voyage, Lewis would draw equipment from the government arsenal at Harper's Ferry, proceed on to Lancaster, Pennsylvania, to practice celestial navigation with Andrew Ellicott, an astronomer who had mapped the upper reaches of the Mississippi, then on to Philadelphia to confer with Jefferson's learned friends there, draw more equipment from the Schuylkill Arsenal, and buy in the local stores whatever the army had been unable to supply. He should be ready to leave for the West by the end of April, and the expedition would start up the Missouri in early summer. If the party met an American vessel at the mouth of the Columbia, it would return by sea. Lewis would communicate through a cypher devised for the President by a Philadelphia mathematician. For some inexplicable reason Jefferson was determined to hide from the world what was already an open secret. In what was perhaps the first calculated lie given the American people by a President, he would tell the press that Lewis was going to explore the upper Mississippi: "It satisfies public curiosity, and masks sufficiently the real destination." Yet the day Congress voted money for the expedition, Jefferson revealed the secret to the British ambassador and four days later to the French ambassador, both of whom gave passports to protect the party if it touched on their countries' territory. (It was to the French ambassador, who asked if Spain had granted a passport, that Jefferson said, "il [sic] devait le donner.")

On March 15 Lewis left for Harper's Ferry, where he planned to stay only a few days. From the arsenal he drew the standard outfit for an army platoon—shoes, stockings, shirts, match coats, woolen overalls, blankets, knapsacks, and hunting shirts. He chose to equip the men with a variety of weapons—muskets, rifles, and blunderbusses—in order to deal with whatever various dangers the wilderness presented. The flintlock musket, although accurate only up to sixty yards, was an adaptable weapon that could be loaded with buckshot, birdshot, or a single ball. The rifle's accuracy extended to at least two hundred yards. Lewis selected the new model the army had been testing, a short-barreled version of the legendary Kentucky rifle. It was easier to carry through the forest, easier to load, and less likely to foul; the reduced barrel only slightly diminished its accuracy. The blunderbuss was a heavy, cumbersome gun with little accuracy, but it produced an awesome report that should impress any troublesome Indians. He planned to mount one on a swivel attached to the prow of the boat. The accountrements for this small arsenal were standard—powder horns and pouches, gun slings, brushes and wires to clean rifle barrels, flints, bullet molds, cartouch boxes to carry paper cartridges filled with "fixed ammunition." He also drew 420 pounds of sheet lead which would be melted down into bullets. The eighteen tomahawks on his manifest were not true tomahawks but small hatchets equipped with hollow handles; with tobacco tamped into the polls they served nicely as pipes.

Lewis collected several items not standard equipment with a typical army unit—forty barbed harpoons to spear fish and beaver; a kit of gunsmith's repair tools; espontoons, an obsolete weapon that once served as a pike but which Lewis favored as a walking stick and gun rest; steel mills for grinding corn, an addition Jefferson suggested as Indian presents.

The expected short stay at Harper's Ferry extended to a month because the blacksmiths had trouble transforming Lewis' line drawings of a pet project into reality. Certain that somewhere along the route the expedition would travel through country without timber, he had designed a collapsible iron frame which, when sheathed with buffalo or elk skins, would serve as a canoe. Days dragged into weeks as the blacksmiths struggled to shape the unique craft to Lewis' specifications. It weighed ninety-nine pounds when finished and Lewis estimated it would carry a load of 1,770 pounds. His creation pleased him immensely.

He counted on spending no more than ten or twelve days in Lancaster practicing celestial observations with Andrew Ellicott, but the lessons went more slowly than expected and three weeks passed before he moved on to Philadelphia, well over a month behind schedule. He stayed in the city nearly six weeks and in the hardware stores, dry goods shops, and apothecaries spend $2,160.14 or all but $340 of what Congress had allotted for the expedition. He ended the shopping tour aware that purchases for the Voyage had barely begun—nearly $4,000 more would be spent before the party moved up the Missouri—but also aware that he had not been spendthrifty. He tucked only a few personal items—a sportsman's whisky flask ($1.50), a pair of pocket pistols ($10.00)—into the purchases. In a book shop he came upon a copy of George Vancouver's account of his cruise to the Pacific Northwest, but instead of buying it—"too costly, and too weighty for me either to purchase or carry"—he stood in the aisle flicking through its pages and noting down what seemed pertinent to his own venture.

The records show that Lewis spent $669.50 on Indian presents —nearly thirty dollars less than the original estimate made when Jefferson was promoting his project with Congress. Among the most expensive items were thirteen pounds of assorted handkerchiefs ($59.83), twenty-two yards of scarlet cloth ($58.50), seventy-three bunches of assorted beads ($41.00), eight and a half pounds of red beads ($25.50), five hundred broaches ($62.07), one hundred thirty rolls of pigtail tobacco ($14.25), forty-eight calico ruffled shirts ($71.04). The thirty gallons of "rectified spirits, such as is used for the Indian trade," ($70.00 plus $7.20 for the six ironbound kegs to store it) listed under *provisions* really belonged under *Indian presents*.

Lewis drew enough from army stores to keep the cost of equipment down to $117.67, nearly $140 less than his original estimate. Under that heading he lumped such items as twelve packages of Castile soap ($1.68), a set of gold scales and weights ($2.33), a black tin saucepan ($1.50). He spent $412.95 on surveying and navigational instruments, over twice what he had planned on. These included a Hadley quadrant ($22.00), a sextant ($90.00), a chronometer ($250.00 plus $.75 for winding keys). He paid $8.00 for a chest to pack these precious instruments in, had it wrapped in canvas, and labeled, *This side up*.

Foresight and imagination led to several purchases for which the expedition would later bless him. He bought eight parcels of catgut material from which to make mosquito curtains ($15.50). He spent $289.50 for one hundred ninety-three pounds of portable soup on the chance the party might, as it did, pass through country empty of game. For $26.25 he bought fifty-two heavy (420 pounds) lead cannisters to carry gunpowder; their screw-on tops made them waterproof, and once empty they could be melted down into bullets. Another multi-purpose item was forty yards of oiled linen "to form two half-faced tents or shelters contrived in such manner their parts may be taken to pieces and again connected at pleasure in order to answer the several purposes of tents, covering to boat or canoe, or if necessary to be used as sails." A frivolous acquisition—a pneumatic rifle or air gun with little power or accuracy—turned out to be one of his happiest. It looked like a Kentucky rifle but produced no loud report or smoke when shot. Astonished Indians would call the mysterious weapon "great medicine" and accord the expedition more than usual respect because of it.

Friends of Jefferson in the city welcomed Lewis during his stay. Dr. Benjamin Rush, Philadelphia's most famous physician, checked over items in the medicine chest and made a few changes. He drew up a list of questions to consider when confronting western Indians ("Do they employ any substitute for ardent spirits to promote intoxication? . . . At what age[s] do the women *begin and cease* to menstruate?") and another list of rules to preserve health in the wilderness. ("Unusual costiveness is often a sign of approaching disease." Take "purging pills" to relieve it. "Flannel should be worn constantly next to the skin, especially in wet weather.") Robert Patterson, a mathematician, guided Lewis' purchases of navigational instruments, prepared tables to help establish latitude and longitude accurately, and suggested textbooks to carry along—Patrick Kelly's *A practical introduction to . . . nautical astronomy . . .* and Nevil Maskelyn's *Tables requisite to be used with the nautical ephermeris for finding the latitude and longitude at sea.* Dr. Benjamin Smith Barton, impetuous, "irritable and even choleric," and known to pass the discoveries of others off as his own, showed his best side to the President's emissary. Lewis bought his *Elements of botany* ($6.oo), a large packet of purple blotting paper, the kind Barton used to press plants, and, probably on Barton's suggestion, translations of Linnaeus' volumes of botanical and zoological classifications. Barton in turn gave Lewis a copy of Antoine Le Page du Pratz's *History of Louisiana*, and probably taught the captain how to preserve plants.

Lewis left Philadelphia for Washington on June 15, pleased with all he had accomplished. He had made astonishingly few mistakes in his purchases. He failed to buy enough or sufficiently strong towing rope. The Indian presents he bought showed he did not know what he was about in this area. He failed, first, to buy enough, and second, to include sufficient blue beads and blue blankets; blue, as he seems not to have known—but any British or French trader did know—was the favorite color with Indians. These were minor misjudgments compared to another decision made in Philadelphia. Lewis decided that instead of a medium-sized boat to carry his expedition up the Missouri he needed one about sixty feet long. Someone or something had convinced him that all the Indians met on his trek might not be as friendly as those Mackenzie encountered. He would, therefore, carry his crew through enemy territory in a floating fortress. The keelboat, as he called it—it had no keel, only a large, pendulous rudder— would be built in Pittsburgh, where there were boat yards accustomed to constructing such crafts for the Ohio River trade. It would carry a load of ten tons, an impossible burden for ten or twelve men to row up any river, let alone the Missouri, known for its swift current. Having opted for the keelboat, Lewis unwittingly broke the pattern set by Mackenzie; his crew must be at least half again the size of the Scotsman's if the cumbersome boat were to move up river. And although Jefferson still spoke of a party of "ten or twelve" to explore the Far West in the elaborate instructions he issued for the Voyage of Discovery on June 20 (three days after Lewis' return to Washington), those instructions shattered the pattern laid down by Mackenzie that up to now both Jefferson and Lewis had been slavishly following.

Chapter 4

The Instructions

Alexander Mackenzie got there. That was his greatest achievement. He crossed the continent and reached the Pacific. Along the way he "could not stop to dig into the earth, over whose surface I was compelled to pass with rapid steps; nor could I turn aside to collect the plants which nature might have scattered on the way. . . ." Jefferson deplored such slipshod procedures and to make sure Lewis did not succumb to them he issued the most demanding set of instructions any explorer up to then had ever been burdened with. The instructions were designed to free Lewis from the tunnel vision that had inhibited Mackenzie, who had studied the land he passed through for its immediate commercial value to England and to him as a fur trader. Captain Lewis took the instructions as orders from his commander-in-chief. Because he obeyed them to the letter what might have been little more than an adventurous trek that got where it was going was transformed into one of the greatest expeditions in this history of exploration.

20 June 1803

To Captain Meriwether Lewis, Esq., captain of the 1st regiment of infantry of the U.S. of A.

Your situation as secretary of the President of the U.S. has made you acquainted with the objects of my confidential message of 18 January 1803 to the legislature. You have seen the act they passed, which, tho' expressed in general terms, was meant to sanction those objects, and you are appointed to carry them into execution.

Instruments for ascertaining, by celestial observations, the geography of the country through which you will pass have already been provided. Light articles for barter and presents among the Indians, arms for your attendants, say from ten to twelve men, boats, tents, and other traveling apparatus, with ammunition, medicine, surgical instruments, and provisions you will have prepared with such aids as the secretary of war can yield in his department. And from him also you will receive authority to engage among our troops, by voluntary agreement, the number of attendants above mentioned, over whom you, as their commanding officer, are invested with all the powers the laws give in such a case.

As your movements while within the limits of the U.S. will be better directed by occasional communications, adapted to the circumstances as they arise, they will be noticed here. What follows will respect your proceedings after your departure from the United States.

Your mission has been communicated to the ministers from France, Spain, and Great Britain, and through them to their governments and such assurances given them as to its objects, as we trust will satisfy them. The country having been ceded by Spain to France the passport you have from the minister of France, the representative of the present sovereign of the country, will be a protection with all its subjects; and that from the minister of England will entitle you to the friendly aid of any traders of that allegiance with whom you may happen to meet.

The object of your mission is to explore the Missouri River

and such principal streams of it, as, by its course and communication with the waters of the Pacific Ocean, whether the Columbia, Oregon, Colorado, or any other river, may offer the most direct and practicable water communication across this continent for the purposes of commerce.

Beginning at the mouth of the Missouri, you will take observations of latitude and longitude at all remarkable points on the river, and especially at the mouths of rivers, at rapids, at islands, and other places and objects distinguished by such natural marks and characters of a durable kind as that they may with certainty be recognized hereafter. The courses of the river between these points of observation may be supplied by the compass, the log line, and by time, corrected by the observations themselves. The variations of the compass, too, in different places should be noticed.

The interesting points of the portage between the heads of the Missouri and of the water offering the best communication with the Pacific Ocean should also be fixed by observation, and the course of that water to the ocean in the same manner as that of the Missouri.

Your observations are to be taken with great pains and accuracy, to be entered distinctly and intelligibly for others as well as yourself to comprehend all the elements necessary, with the aid of the usual tables, to fix the latitude and longitude of the places at which they were taken, and are to be rendered to the war office for the purpose of having the calculations made concurrently by proper persons within the U.S. Several copies of these, as well as your notes, should be made at leisure times, and put into the care of the most trustworthy of your attendants, to guard, by multiplying them, against the accidental losses to which they will be exposed. A further guard would be that one of these copies be on the paper of the birch, as less liable to injury from damp than common paper.

The commerce which may be carried on with the people inhabiting the line you will pursue renders a knowledge of those people important. You will therefore endeavor to make yourself acquainted, as far as a diligent pursuit of your journey shall admit, with the names of the nations and their numbers:

the extent and limits of their possessions;

their relations with other tribes or nations;

their language, traditions, monuments;

their ordinary occupations in agriculture, fishing, hunting, war, arts, and the implements for these;

their food, clothing, and domestic accommodations;

the diseases prevalent among them and the remedies they use;

moral and physical circumstances which distinguish them from the tribes we know;

pecularities in their laws, customs, and dispositions; and

articles of commerce they may need or furnish and to what extent.

And considering the interest which every nation has in extending and strengthening the authority of reason and justice among the people around them, it will be useful to acquire what knowledge you can of the state of morality, religion, and information among them; as it may better enable those who may endeavor to civilize and instruct them, to adapt their measures to the existing notions and practices of those on whom they are to operate.

Other objects worthy of notice will be:

the soil and face of the country, its growth and vegetable productions, especially those not of the U.S.;

the animals of the country generally, and especially those not known in the U.S.;

the remains or accounts of any which may be deemed rare or extinct;

the mineral productions of every kind; but more particularly metals, limestone, pit coal, and saltpeter; salines and minerals waters, noting the temperature of the last, and such circumstances as may indicate their character;

volcanic appearances;

climate, as characterized by the thermometer, by the proportion of rainy, cloudy, and clear days, by lightning, hail,

snow, ice, by the access and recess of frost, by the winds
prevailing at different seasons, the dates at which particular plants put forth or lose their flower or leaf, times of
appearance of particular birds, reptiles, or insects.

Altho' your route will be along the channel of the Missouri,
yet you will endeavor to inform yourself by inquiry of the character
and extent of the country watered by its branches, and especially
on its southern side. The North River or Rio Bravo, which runs
into the Gulf of Mexico, and the North River or Rio Colorado,
which runs into the Gulf of California, are understood to be the
principal streams heading opposite to the waters of the Missouri,
and running southwardly. Whether the dividing grounds between
the Missouri and them are mountains or flat lands, what are their
distance from the Missouri, the character of the intermediate
country, and the people inhabiting it, are worthy of particular inquiry. The northern waters of the Missouri are less to be inquired
after, because they have been ascertained to a considerable degree
and are still in a course of ascertainment by English traders and
travelers. But if you can learn anything certain of the most northern source of the Mississippi and of its position relatively to the
Lake of the Woods, it will be interesting to us.

Some account, too, of the path of the Canadian traders from
the Mississippi at the mouth of the Ouisconsing [Wisconsin] to
where it strikes the Missouri and of the soil and rivers in its course
is desirable.

In all your intercourse with the natives treat them in the most
friendly and conciliatory manner which their own conduct will
admit. Allay all jealousies as to the object of your journey, satisfy
them of its innocence, make them acquainted with the position,
extent, character, peaceable, and commercial dispositions of the
U.S., of our wish to be neighborly, friendly, and useful to them,
and of our disposition to a commercial intercourse with them.
Confer with them on the points most convenient as mutual em-
poriums and the articles of most desirable interchange for them
and us. If a few of their influential chiefs, within practicable dis-

tance, wish to visit us, arrange such a visit with them, and furnish
them with authority to call on our officers, on their entering the
U.S., to have them convey to this place at the public expense. If
any of them should wish to have some of their young people
brought up with us and taught such arts as may be useful to them,
we will receive, instruct, and take care of them. Such a mission,
whether of influential chiefs or of young people, would give some
security to your own party. Carry with you some matter of the
kine pox; inform those of them with whom you may be of its
efficacy as a preservative from the smallpox, and instruct and encourage them in the use of it. This may be especially done
wherever you winter.

As it is impossible for us to foresee in what manner you will
be received by those people, whether with hospitality or hostility,
so is it impossible to prescribe the exact degree of perseverance
with which you are to pursue your journey. We value too much
the lives of citizens to offer them to probable destruction. Your
numbers will be sufficient to secure you against the unauthorized
opposition of individuals or of small parties. But if a superior force,
authorized or not authorized, by a nation should be arrayed against
your further passage, and inflexibly determined to arrest it, you
must decline its farther pursuit and return. In the loss of yourselves
we should lose also the information you will have acquired. By
returning safely with that, you may enable us to renew the essay
with better calculated means. To your own discretion therefore
must be left the degree of danger you may risk, and the point at
which you should decline, only saying we wish you to err on the
side of your safety, and to bring back your party safe even if it be
with less information.

As far up the Missouri as the white settlements extend, an
intercourse will probably be found to exist between them and the
Spanish posts of Saint Louis opposite Cahokia, or Ste. Genevieve
opposite Kaskakia. From still further up the river, the traders may
furnish a conveyance for letters. Beyond that, you may perhaps be
able to engage Indians to bring letters for the government to

Cahokia or Kaskaskia, on promising that they shall there receive such special compensation as you shall have stipulated with them. Avail yourself of these means to communicate to us, at seasonable intervals, a copy of your journal, notes, and observations of every kind, putting into cypher whatever might do injury if betrayed.

Should you reach the Pacific Ocean, inform yourself of the circumstances which may decide whether the furs of those parts may not be collected as advantageously at the head of the Missouri (convenient, as is supposed, to the waters of the Colorado and Oregon or Columbia) as at Nootka Sound or any other point of that coast; and that trade be consequently conducted through the Missouri and U.S. more beneficially than by the circumnavigation now practiced.

On your arrival on that coast endeavor to learn if there be any port within your reach frequented by the sea vessels of any nation, and to send two of your trusty people back by sea, in such way as shall appear practicable, with a copy of your notes. And should you be of opinion that the return of your party by the way they went will be eminently dangerous, then ship the whole and return by sea, by the way either of Cape Horn or the Cape of Good Hope, as you shall be able. As you will be without money, clothes, or provisions, you must endeavor to use the credit of the U.S. to obtain them, for which purpose open letters of credit shall be furnished you, authorizing you to draw upon the executive of the U.S. or any of its officers in any part of the world, on which draughts can be disposed of, and to apply with our recommendations to the consuls, agents, merchants, or citizens of any nation with which we have intercourse, assuring them, in our name, that any aids they may furnish you shall be honorably repaid, and on demand. Our consuls Thomas Hewes at Batavia in Java, William Buchanan in the Isles of France and Bourbon, and John Elmslie at the Cape of Good Hope will be able to supply your necessities by draughts on us.

Should you find it safe to return by the way you go, after sending two of your party round by sea, or with the whole party, if no conveyance by sea can be found, do so; making such observations on your return as may serve to supply, correct, or confirm those made on your outward journey.

On re-entering the U.S. and reaching a place of safety, discharge any of your attendants who may desire and deserve it, procuring for them immediate payment of all arrears of pay and clothing which may have incurred since their departure, and assure them that they shall be recommended to the liberality of the legislature for the grant of a soldier's portion of land each, as proposed in my message to Congress. And repair yourself with your papers to the seat of government.

To provide on the accident of your death against anarchy, dispersion, and consequent danger to your party, and total failure of the enterprise, you are hereby authorized, by any instrument signed and written in your own hand, to name the person among them who shall succeed to the command on your decease, and by like instruments to change the nomination from time to time as further experience of the characters accompanying you shall point out superior fitness. And all the powers and authorities given to yourself are, in the event of your death, transferred to and vested in the successor so named, with further power to him and his successors in like manner to name each his successor, who, on the death of his predecessor, shall be invested with all the powers and authorities given to yourself.

Given under my hand at the city of Washington this 20th day of June 1803.

THOMAS JEFFERSON, PRESIDENT
UNITED STATES OF AMERICA

Chapter 5

Permutations

Jefferson's instructions told Lewis he must not only lead the expedition on its long trek through the unknown, overseeing day-to-day operations; he must also conduct diplomatic negotiations with all redmen and whites (French, Spanish, and British) met along the way and simultaneously serve as the party's cartographer, mineralogist, ethnologist, botanist, zoologist, meterologist, and geographer. Lewis read an early draft of the instructions while in Philadelphia and it must have then struck him the President had placed upon him responsibilities too great for one man to carry out successfully. On June 19, two days after returning to Washington, he sent William Clark, the younger brother of George Rogers Clark, an invitation to join the expedition. "I make this communication to you with the privity of the President, who expresses an anxious wish that you would consent to join me in the enterprise. He has authorized me to say that in the event of your accepting this proposition he will grant you a captain's commission.

. . . Your situation, if joined with me in this mission, will in all respects be precisely such as my own."

Jefferson's letter may have persuaded Lewis to take on a co-commander. When drawing up the instructions the President had asked the cabinet for advice. Levi Lincoln, the attorney general, offered several suggestions—among them, that the party should carry along kine pox to vaccinate the Indians—and one concerned Lewis. "From my idea of Capt. Lewis, he will be much more likely, in case of difficulty, to push too far, than to recede too soon. Would it not be well to change the term 'certain to destruction' into 'probable destruction' and to add that these dangers are never to be encountered, which vigilance, precaution, and attention can secure against, at a reasonable expense." While incorporating this advice into the revised instructions, it may have occurred to Jefferson that Lewis' "undaunted courage" would, unchecked, carry the expedition to disaster. Surely it would do no harm to have a companion of probity along to rein him in when the situation called for restraint.

For ten years, so he later said, Lewis had dreamed of the glory of being the first man to reach the Pacific by way of the Missouri. He did not wish to share that glory with a co-commander. Ideally, he wanted an executive officer to take charge of the expedition's daily affairs, leaving Lewis still in command but free to perform the other assignments handed him by the President. But Lewis knew Clark would not join the party as a subordinate. He was four years older than Lewis and had outranked him when the two served together in the army. Since then he had resigned his commission and returned home to Clarksville, in the Indiana Territory, to manage his lands there and to put in order the affairs of his famous brother, who had deteriorated into an alcoholic. Few in the Northwest Territory had heard of Meriwether Lewis, but William Clark's fame, at the age of thirty-three, was exceeded only by his brother's. When Henry Dearborn, the secretary of war, in 1802 wanted to build a fort at the mouth of the Ohio, he wrote Clark for advice.

William Clark, painting by Charles Willson Peale
INDEPENDENCE NATIONAL HISTORICAL PARK COLLECTION

Clark's presence, unlike Lewis', caused people to turn their heads when he came down the road. He was over six feet tall. He had a shock of red hair but lacked the temper commonly associated with it. He was an amiable man, admired by all who worked with him, and known to be "brave as Caesar." During an Indian uprising a companion remarked that "in the kind of warfare in which we are engaged I had rather have him with me than any other man in the United States." He differed from other Indian fighters in that the natives liked and trusted him. He was at ease in the forest but also an experienced riverman who had traveled from his home along the Ohio down the Mississippi and back. He was a cartographer of considerable ability, although self-trained, and also an artist who could make incredibly accurate likenesses of whatever he fixed his eye upon. He thought himself poorly educated, but anyone who could compare the antelope of the western plains to the "gazelle of Africa," who could remark on an Indian's "aquiline nose," or speak of an endemic eye disease among western tribes "as almost invariably a concomitant of old age," was better educated than his wildly imaginative spelling indicated. George Rogers Clark summed up his brother's talents nicely: "He is well qualified almost for any business."

Lewis' letter to Clark mentioned that France now owned the Louisiana Territory but that "very sanguine expectations are at this time formed by our government that the whole of that immense country watered by the Mississippi and its tributary streams, Missouri inclusive, will be the property of the United States in less than twelve months from this date." Even so, Lewis saw no reason to abandon what remained of his fractured time schedule. He still planned to get seven or eight hundred miles up the Missouri before winter set in and would leave Pittsburgh as soon as he had cleared up loose ends in Washington.

Albert Gallatin, secretary of the treasury, had shown particular interest in the expedition, and before leaving Washington Lewis visited him to collect a map of the Far West which Gallatin had commissioned. The cartographer, Nicholas King, had drawn

on all information then in the public domain—Ellicott's map of
the upper Mississippi, Vancouver's of the lower Columbia, Aaron
Arrowsmith's of western Canada to the Pacific, and the work of
two Frenchmen, Jean Baptiste d'Anville and Guillaume Delisle.
Even so, King's handiwork pinpointed with certainty only three
spots along the expedition's prospective route—the mouth of the
Missouri, the site of the Mandan villages, where British and French
traders were a constant presence, and the lower Columbia. The
rest remained a huge blank for the Voyage of Discovery to fill in.

From the War Department Lewis collected a box of medals
to be distributed among Indian chiefs. They were of several grades.
Two carried Jefferson's portrait and were for greater and lesser
chiefs; the larger of these was slightly over three inches in diameter.
Two other smaller ones were emblazoned with domestic animals
and with a farmer sowing grain. (The "sowing medals," as Lewis
called them, showed the War Department's thrifty side; they were
left over from Washington's presidency.) The department also
gave him a stack of certificates to be passed out among Indian
chiefs. When signed by Lewis or Clark they attested that the chief
who had received one had given abundant proof of "his amicable
disposition to cultivate peace, harmony, and good neighborhood
with the said States . . . the government of which will at all times
be extended to their protection, so long as they do acknowledge
the authority of the same." The department also gave Lewis a supply of flags of varying sizes to pass out among the tribes.

Lewis had planned to leave for Pittsburgh by the end of June
when a rumor floated in that the sale of Louisiana to the United
States had been completed. He lingered in Washington for confirmation, which came on July 3. The next day he and the President celebrated what both must have thought the most glorious
and momentous Fourth of July since 1776.

Lewis departed early the following morning. He paused at
Harper's Ferry and "shot my guns and examined the several articles
which had been manufactured for me at this place; they appear to
be well executed." He reached Pittsburgh on July 15 to find that

the keelboat would not be ready for at least three weeks. Seven passed before he could leave. He visited the boat yard daily but his officious presence did nothing to speed and perhaps helped to retard progress: "neither threats, entreaties, nor any other mode of treatment which I could devise had any effect." The region suffered from a severe dry spell and each day Lewis watched the Ohio's level drop perceptibly. His fear that the river would soon be too low to carry the keelboat, which had a draft of three feet when empty, four when loaded, convinced him to purchase "two or three pirogues and descend the river in them and depend on purchasing a boat as I descended." Knowledgeable natives said he would never find a boat the size he wanted further down the Ohio, which left him at the mercy of the boat yard's "incorrigible drunkards."

He filled gaps in his stores while waiting—eighteen more axes, a portable blacksmith forge, a supply of iron and steel sheets from which to shape parts for worn out equipment. A squad of soldiers recruited from the post at Carlisle, Pennsylvania, arrived to take the boat down river. And from Clark came an amiable letter accepting Lewis' invitation. "This is an undertaking freighted with many difficulties, but, my friend, I do assure you that no man lives with whom I would prefer to undertake such a trip, etc., as yourself."

Molasses in winter moved faster than the boat yard's carpenters. It took them twelve days just to make the poles and twenty-two oars for the keelboat. Finally, at 7 A.M. August 31, the builder announced the boat finished—his bill came to $900, about twice what Lewis had planned on—and the captain had it loaded immediately. The party set out three hours later, guided by a pilot who for $70 would take them to the Falls of the Ohio, where Clark awaited. The low river had forced Lewis to send part of his load by wagon down to Wheeling, Virginia.

Little went right on the trip down the Ohio. Lewis' journal gave a poignant record of mishaps. A few miles below Pittsburgh he showed off the air gun to a crowd on shore. One shot struck a woman in the audience. "She fell instantly, the blood gushing from her temple. We were all in the greatest consternation, and supposed she was dead, but in a minute she revived, to our inexpressible satisfaction, and by examination we found the wound by no means mortal or even dangerous." The next day Lewis had to hire a team of horses to pull the boat over a riffle. Local inhabitants preyed on river travelers and charged them extravagantly—two dollars per riffle—"when they are called on for assistance and have no philanthropy or conscience." A few days later he reached Wheeling, where the wagon sent ahead was waiting with its load in good order. There Lewis purchased a pirogue, as westerners called it—a large flat-bottom boat. He transferred the wagon's load and some of the keelboat's into it and proceeded on. The crew now gave trouble. Some displeased Lewis and he fired them, others found the labor too much and quit. At one layover two of the men were so drunk they had to be helped aboard. Gravel bars often gave the boat no more than six inches of water and only after the crew had jumped out with shovels and cut a sluice that the river soon scoured into a channel could the boat slide through.

On September 28, the party reached Cincinnati, nearly five hundred miles downriver from Pittsburgh but still over a hundred miles from Clarksville at the Falls of the Ohio. Here, surrounded by the turning leaves of autumn, Lewis faced up to a decision he had avoided for weeks—the days had dribbled away and there no longer remained enough traveling time to move up the Missouri this year. Instead, because Congress must be kept "in a good humor on the subject of the expedition"—the season of duty in Washington had taught him to be sensitive to congressional whims —"I have concluded to make a tour this winter on horseback of some hundred miles through the most interesting portion of the country adjoining my winter establishment" at the mouth of the Missouri.

Jefferson's instructions would set the tone for all that would follow, but up to this point he had made only restrained comments on preparations for the expedition. When Lewis lingered a month at Harper's Ferry fussing over his iron boat, the President had only said, "I have no doubt you have used every possible exertion to get off, and therefore we have only to lament what cannot be helped, as the delay of a month now may lose a year in the end." But this proposal from Cincinnati of a solitary winter tour of the Indian country flanking the lower reaches of the Missouri provoked a response that made clear who ran the expedition as long as it remained in touch with Washington. "One thing . . . we are decided in," Jefferson told Lewis—"that you must not undertake the winter excursion which you propose in yours of October 3. Such an excursion will be more dangerous than the main expedition up the Missouri, and would, by an accident to you, hazard our main object, which, since the acquisition of Louisiana, interests everybody in the highest degree. The object of your mission is single, the direct water communication from sea to sea. . . ." The President must have thanked God that by the time his letter arrived Lewis had joined up with Clark at the Falls of the Ohio.

Chapter 6

Camp Wood

On October 15, when he joined up with Clark below the Falls of the Ohio, Lewis began to shed some of the burden he had carried for nearly a year. Preparations now moved into a second stage—recruitment of candidates for the permanent party. When the captains set out from Clarksville they had sorted out a nucleus of nine men whom they enlisted in the army for five years or for the duration of the expedition. Each of the men received a bounty of twelve dollars for signing up. Their names were: William E. Bratton, John Colter, Joseph and Reuben Field, Charles Floyd, Jr., George Gibson, Nathaniel H. Pryor, George Shannon, and John Shields. A tenth member of the party was Clark's paunchy slave, York, who would serve as cook and orderly for the leaders.

All western army posts had been alerted by the War Department to collect volunteers for the expedition, and from November 11, when the boats reached Fort Massac, thirty-five miles up from the mouth of the Ohio, until late December, the party's provisional roster slowly increased. Fort Massac produced two men; Kaskaskia, ten; Cahokia, six; and South West Point, Tennessee, nine whom Clark did not think much of. The prize recruit was George Drouillard; the captains spelled his name as they pronounced it—Drewyer. His mother was a Shawnee and his father a French-Canadian frontiersman. Out of this mixed heritage had come a superb hunter, trapper, and scout, but the captains wanted him mainly for his knowledge of the Indian "language of gesticulation." They invited him to join the party as interpreter, a civilian post that would pay twenty-five dollars a month, the salary of a second lieutenant. Drouillard accepted the invitation provisionally, and not until the end of December, after he had sized up the leaders and decided the expedition had a chance to survive, did he definitely agree to sign on.

The party spent the next half year—from early December until mid-May—camped on the east side of the Mississippi opposite the mouth of the Missouri along a small stream the French called Dubois and the Americans renamed Wood River. Clark ran Camp Wood while Lewis funneled supplies and provisions to the party from his headquarters in Saint Louis. Lewis always called it "my expedition" in his correspondence. Citizens of Saint Louis and President Jefferson called it "Captain Lewis' expedition." But for the men at Camp Wood it was as much, if not more, Clark's expedition. It was he who took a disparate band of raw recruits from scattered army posts and shaped them into a tightly-knit crew. It was he who guided them through the first hard weeks at Camp Wood when they lived in tents while building cabins to protect them from the cold. They lived on a thin diet those early days, for the hunters found that the local settlers had stripped the countryside of game. Once in desperation the hunters brought in a haunch found hanging from a tree and tried to pass it off on Clark as bear meat. Next day he sent out a man "to inquire in the neighborhood whose hog it was." He depended too much on neighboring farmers to antagonize them. One had hired out his team to haul logs for the cabins. Others brought in loads of corn, turnips, butter and eggs, potatoes and chickens, some for sale, some as gifts. These helped carry the party nicely through the early weeks until Lewis had arranged for the purveyor's supplies to start flowing in.

Early in the morning on December 25 Clark was jolted awake with "a Christmas discharge and found that of the party [that] had got drunk two fought. The men frolicked and hunted all day." A few days later all the cabins were finished and with time on their hands the men settled down to serious drinking. Clark tried to relieve the tedium with a series of shooting matches between his party and men from the neighborhood. He offered a silver dollar to the winner of the first contest, then had to watch sadly as "the country people won the dollar." But a few weeks later he could report that "several country men came to win my men's money; in doing so lost all they had with them," and by early May the country people in every match "all get beat and lose their money." But drunkenness remained a continual problem. Army regulations allowed every man a gill of whisky a day, half in the morning, half in the evening. In one month the party drank 538 rations or some 130 quarts from the official stores, but this consumption, modest for some thirty men accustomed to hard drinking, was supplemented by an endless supply of bootleg whisky. Early on Clark "issued orders and prohibited a certain Ramey from selling liquor to the party," but the Rameys continued to infiltrate the camp with their rotgut. Regularly Clark had to admit in his journal, "several men confined for drunkenness today" or "several drunk."

Clark disbursed work assignments informally and rarely bothered with written orders of the day. When Lewis took charge while his partner enjoyed a holiday in Saint Louis, things changed abruptly.

20 February 1804

The commanding officer directs that during the absence of himself and Captain Clark from camp that the party shall consider themselves under the immediate command of Sergeant Ordway, who will be held accountable for the good police and order of the camp during that period, and will also see the subsequent parts of this order carried into effect.

The sawyers will continue their work until they have cut the necessary quantity of plank. The quantity wanting will be determined by Pryor. During the days they labor they shall receive each an extra gill of whisky per day and be exempt from guard duty; when the work is accomplished they will join the party and do duty in common with the other men.

The blacksmiths will also continue their work until they have completed the articles contained in the memorandum with which I have furnished them, and during the time they are at work they will receive each an extra gill of whisky per day and be exempt from guard duty; when the work is completed they will return to camp and do duty in common with the detachment.

The four men who are engaged in making sugar will continue in that employment until further orders and will receive each a half a gill of extra whisky per day and be exempt from guard duty.

The practicing party will in future discharge only one round each per day, which will be done under the direction of Sergeant Ordway, all at the same target and at the distance of fifty yards off hand. The prize of a gill of extra whisky will be received by the person who makes the best shot at each time of practice.

Floyd will take charge of our quarters and store and be exempt from guard duty until our return. The commanding officer hopes that this proof of his confidence will be justified by the rigid performance of the orders given him on that subject.

No man shall absent himself from camp without the knowledge and permission of Sergeant Ordway, other than those who have obtained permission from me to be absent on hunting excursions, and those will not extend their absence to a term by which they may avoid a tour of guard duty. On their return they will report themselves to Sergeant Ordway and receive his instructions.

No whisky shall in future be delivered from the contractor's store except for the legal ration and as appropriated by this order, unless otherwise directed by Captain Clark or myself.

MERIWETHER LEWIS, CAPTAIN
1ST. U.S. REGULAR INFANTRY

Lewis' next order, really a lecture, revealed a man who had been much put upon the past few days.

3 March 1804

The commanding officer feels himself mortified and disappointed at the disorderly conduct of Reuben Field in refusing to mount guard when in the due routine of duty he was regularly warned. Nor is he less surprised at the want of discretion in those who urged his opposition to the faithful discharge of his duty, particularly Shields, whose sense of propriety he had every reason to believe would have induced him rather to have promoted good order than to have excited disorder and faction among the party, particularly in the absence of Captain Clark and himself. The commanding officer is also sorry to find any man who has been engaged by himself and Captain Clark for the expedition on which they have entered so destitute of understanding as not to be able to draw the distinction between being placed under the command of another officer whose will in such case would be their law and that of obeying the orders of Captain Clark and himself communicated to them through Sergeant Ordway, who, as one of the party, has during their necessary absence been charged with the execution of their orders; acting from those orders expressly and not from his own caprice and who is in all respects accountable to us for the faithful observance of the same.

A moment's reflection must convince every man of our party that were we to neglect the more important and necessary arrangements in relation to the voyage we are now entering on, for the purpose merely of remaining at camp in order to communicate our orders in person to the individuals of the party on mere points of police, they would have too much reason to complain. Nay, even to fear the ultimate success of the enterprise in which we are all embarked. The abuse of some of the party with respect to the privilege heretofore granted them of going into the country, is not less displeasing; to such as have made hunting or other business a pretext to cover their design of visiting a neighboring whisky shop, he cannot for the present extend this privilege; and does therefore most postively direct that Colter, Boyle, Wiser, and Robinson do not receive permission to leave camp under any pretext whatever for ten days, after this order is read on the parade, unless otherwise directed hereafter by Captain Clark or himself. The commanding officers highly approve of the conduct of Sergeant Ordway.

The carpenters, blacksmiths, and in short the whole party (except Floyd, who has been specially directed to perform other duties) are to obey implicitly the orders of Sergeant Ordway, who has received our instructions on these subjects and is held accountable to us for their execution.

MERIWETHER LEWIS, CAPTAIN

1ST U.S. REGULAR INFANTRY

COMMANDING DETACHMENT

While Lewis passed out orders at Camp Wood, Jefferson did the same from Washington. He reminded Lewis that "The object of your mission is single, the direct water communication from sea to sea formed by the bed of the Missouri and perhaps the Oregon [i.e., Columbia]." The treaty of cession with France defined the boundaries of the Louisiana Territory as "the high lands enclosing all the waters which run into the Mississippi or Missouri directly or indirectly." Thus, it was crucial "to fix with precision by celestial observations the longitude and latitude of the sources of these rivers, . . . furnishing points in the contour of our new limits." Finally, Lewis must remember his mission is of "major importance and therefore not to be delayed or hazarded by any episodes whatever."

From afar Jefferson helped where he could to prepare Lewis and Clark for the journey ahead. He sent a compact edition of

Mackenzie's trek across Canada; a copy of a journal by Jean Baptiste Truteau, who had lived among the Arikara Indians on the Missouri; a copy of a map of the Missouri by John Evans, which covered sixteen hundred miles of the river from Saint Louis to the Mandan villages. William Henry Harrison, governor of the Indiana Territory, forwarded another map of the Missouri—this one drawn by James Mackay. His gift was superfluous, for Mackay still lived in the vicinity of Saint Louis. He visited Camp Wood and helped to refine Clark's first draft of the Missouri's course. Mackay told him that "a beautiful country presents itself. . . ."

On March 9, the captains attended the formal transfer of Upper Louisiana from Spain to France and from France to the United States. When the Spanish flag was lowered and that of France was run up the pole, the largely French audience, moved to see the tricolor waving overhead for the first time in forty-one years, begged to let it fly overnight. The request was granted and not until the next day did all the land drained by the Missouri and its tributaries become American.

By now the ice had begun to break up in the rivers. Preparations for departure moved into the final stage. The carpenters built a second pirogue when it became apparent that the mounds of supplies and provisions heaped about the camp would not fit into the two boats brought down the Ohio. Clark redesigned the keelboat topside, installing a thirty-two foot jointed mast for a sail, ridgepoles to hold an awning to shield the oarsmen, and a line of lockers whose hinged tops when raised would serve as a breastwork against Indian attacks. A small cannon on the prow of the keelboat and blunderbusses for the pirogues, all on swivels, were also added.

On March 31, the captains made their final selections for "the detachment destined for the expedition through the interior of the continent of North America." The men picked, in addition to the nine who had enlisted at the Falls of the Ohio, were:

John Collins	*Silas Goodrich*
Patrick Gass	*Hugh Hall*

Thomas P. Howard	John B. Thompson
Hugh McNeal	William Werner
John Newman	Joseph Whitehouse
John Ordway	Alexander H. Willard
John Potts	Richard Windsor
Moses B. Reed	Peter M. Wiser

The permanent party of twenty-two privates and three sergeants—Ordway, Pryor, and Floyd—would man the keelboat. The sergeants would get fifteen dollars a month, the privates ten, and after the expedition all would receive "at least four hundred acres of first-rate land and if we make great discoveries, as we expect, the United States has promised to make us great rewards, more than we are promised, etc." A temporary party of six privates under Corporal Richard Warfington would take the small pirogue up to the Mandan villages and bring the keelboat back to Saint Louis. They would receive only their army pay for carrying out the assignment.

The party planned to set out in mid-April, but once again the timetable fell apart. The large pirogue still lacked a crew and did not get one until early May when Auguste Chouteau, a Saint Louis fur trader who with his brother Pierre had been especially helpful in preparing Lewis and Clark for their voyage into the unknown, produced eight engagés, led by their patroon Baptiste Deschamps, who were willing to take the boat as far as the Mandan villages. Lewis tried to bargain over the salaries—something like twice that of an army private—but "found it impossible to reduce them." Chouteau probably also turned up the two experienced rivermen who agreed to serve as the keelboat's pilots—Pierre Cruzatte and François Labiche. They both took what was for French voyageurs an extraordinary step—they enlisted as privates in the United States Army for the length of the voyage.

By now Camp Wood looked like a supply depot prepared to outfit an army, not just a crew of some thirty men. The job of compressing the mountains of stores into barrels and bales and boxes fell to Clark. In mid-April, after he had packed fifty barrels of pork and "rolled and filled them with brine," he took stock of what was ready for loading into the boats, giving the weight in pounds for each item.

14 bags of parched meal	1200
9 bags of common meal	800
11 bags of hulled corn	1000
30 barrels of flour	3900
7 bags and 4 barrels of biscuits	650
7 barrels of salt	870
50 kegs of pork	4500
2 boxes of candles and soap	170
1 bag of candlewicks	8
1 bag of coffee	50
1 bag of beans and 1 of peas	100
2 bags of sugar	112
1 keg of hog's lard	100
4 barrels of hulled corn	650
1 barrel of meal	170
grease	600

At this point, without bothering to total the weight, Clark drifted into generalities—21 bales of Indian goods, "tools of every description, etc., etc." Before any of this was loaded into the boats the purveyor's agent at Clark's request "was polite enough to examine all my provisions; several kegs of pork he condemned."

A few days later John Hay, a former fur trader, came over from Cahokia to help Clark out. During his years of traveling among the Indians he had learned a number of tricks about how to pack for the wilderness that he now passed on to Clark. Never, for example, fill a box or a bale with a single item from your supplies. Thus the contents of a typical bale of the seven bales of "necessary stores" packed under Hay's supervision were: four blankets, three fine cloth jackets, six flannel shirts, three pairs of overalls, five frocks, four white shirts, two hundred flints, two spike gimlets, two small gimlets, twelve pairs of socks, two tin boxes containing two memorandum books each, a half pound of colored thread, one roman handkerchief, one piece of catgut, three sets of rifle locks, one screw driver.

A bag, typical of the fourteen packed full of Indian presents under Hay's direction, contained the following: for the first chief, a scarlet coat, a hat with feather, a white shirt, a pair of scarlet leggings, a breech clout, a large medal, a small bundle of garters, a silver moon, a wrist band, an arm band, and a flag; for the chief's wife, a roll of ribbon and a silk handkerchief; for the second chief, a blue blanket and a smaller medal; for the third chief, a still smaller medal, a breech clout, shirt, leggings, and garters; for "some great man" in the tribe, a callico shirt; for "some considered man," a tomahawk; for "some woman of consideration," an ivory comb; for the women generally, bunches of thread, garters, varied colored beads, 412 needles, 61 fish hooks, a half dozen iron combs, some glass ear bobs, six silver rings, nine pair of scissors; for the men, burning glasses, a dozen knives, five looking glasses, one hundred broaches, fifty moccasin awls, a half dozen Jews' harps, three razors.

Only a wild guess can be made what all this and hundreds of other unlisted items weighed. Clark's far from complete figures totaled up to nearly twenty-one thousand pounds. They did not include the weight of the load brought from Harper's Ferry, the portable blacksmith shop and its supply of bar iron and horseshoes, the kegs of whisky and brandy, the men's personal luggage, the bales of Indian presents and "necessary stores." Regardless of the final tally, the men knew from the moment they pulled on the oars they had an awful lot of cargo to row up a far from lazy river.

Early in May while Clark was loading the boats, a letter came to him from Lewis in Saint Louis. In it was Clark's commission from the secretary of war. The War Department had downgraded him from the captaincy promised to second lieutenant. The cause for the demotion lay with Jefferson, who, so far as the record shows, made no effort to force the War Department to live up to the bargain made. Indeed, he appears to have gone out of his way to keep Clark inferior in rank. In the President's mind the Voyage of

Discovery was Captain Lewis' expedition and "Lieut. Clark was appointed second in command." So he told Congress in his first report on the voyage's progress.

The news from Washington disturbed Lewis. "It is not such as I wished, or had reason to expect," he wrote Clark, "but so it is. . . . I think it will be best to let none of our party or any other persons know anything about the grade. You will observe that the grade has no effect upon your compensation, which by G—d shall be equal to my own." (It was not. Lewis as captain received $480 a year, Clark as lieutenant $360, and there is no record that Lewis did anything to equalize the compensation.) "I did not think myself very well treated," Clark said later, but the broken promise did not affect his relations with Lewis or the men, who never learned his true rank and always called him Captain. Throughout the expedition he stood "in point of rank and command with Captain Lewis—*equal in every point of view.*"

Part Two

Upriver

Chapter 7

Shakedown

Clark's eagerness to test the men and boats on a trial run to Saint Charles, some twenty miles upstream, led to a departure from Camp Wood on 14 May 1804, a day ahead of schedule. All the people in the neighborhood came down to give the party a send-off. The two pirogues, with the American colors flying from their prows, moved out first—the engagés in one, Corporal Warfington and his squad of six soldiers in the other. The keelboat—the men called it the barge, an apter name for the ponderous craft—carried Clark, the sergeants, and twenty-two soldiers at the oars; Cruzatte, the pilot, with his assistant Labiche stood in the bow. The hunters moved ahead by land with the four horses.

It took two days for the caravan of neophytes to reach Saint Charles, a village of some 450 "dressy, polite" people of French descent. The citizens had planned a ball for the crew that night. Before letting the men go Clark reminded all that if they lacked "a true respect for their own dignity" they would soon find them-

Breakfast at Sunrise, watercolor by Alfred Jacob Miller

selves in "a more retired situation," that is, homeward bound. The agreeable evening "dancing with the French ladies" did not satisfy Warner and Hall, who stayed out all night, or Collins, who went to the ball without permission, behaved there "in an unbecoming manner," and upon returning spoke to Clark in a way "to bring into disrespect the orders of the commanding officer." Next day a courtmartial composed of four of their peers found Warner and Hall guilty, sentenced them to twenty-five lashes "on their naked back," but recommended mercy because of "their former good conduct." Clark remanded the sentences. The court found Collins guilty of all charges and sentenced him to fifty lashes; the crew administered the punishment at sunset.

The party stayed five days at Saint Charles, taking aboard more supplies—fresh eggs and butter, milk, corn, bacon, freshly baked bread and biscuits—and shifting loads to make the boats more stable. On Sunday, May 20, most of the men went to church, although the village had only a Catholic mass to offer their Protestant souls. This was the last time they would observe the Sabbath for over two years; exploring the Missouri and points farther west would be a seven-day-a-week operation. That afternoon Lewis rode in with a party of gentlemen from Saint Louis and the next afternoon, "We set out from this place, fired our bow piece and gave three cheers, and proceeded on in good heart." They moved only a mile upstream, just far enough to put the temptations of Saint Charles' women behind for all except three of the *engagés* who did not rejoin the party until next morning. (A few weeks later one of them came down with venereal disease.)

A desultory pace marked the early days on the river as the men adjusted to their oars. They paused at a settlement founded by Daniel Boone, who may have been among the spectators when the boats landed for an hour to buy some corn and butter. A mile farther along they inspected a large cave. A scattering of names were written on the rock and Clark for the first of many times during the next two years added "mine among others." An hour or so later they picked up Lewis who, while walking on shore had nearly tumbled from a cliff but saved himself by digging his knife into the soil. Clark spent most of the early days on the barge, but when he walked on shore he sometimes made an incongruously dainty sight carrying an umbrella to shield himself from the blistering sun.

Within a week the river had exposed a catalogue of treacheries. The current—so swift it was "impossible to resist its force by means of oars or poles in the main channel"—astonished them. When the banks were firm the men jumped ashore and pulled the boats upstream by ropes. All agreed this was "the safest and most expeditious mode of traveling, except with sails in a steady and favorable breeze." If the ropes or cords, as the men called them, could not be used, Cruzatte or Labiche whenever possible sought eddies along the river's edges. But there the boats faced the danger of falling banks. The scouring river constantly ate away the fine soil that lined the river's edges. "It happens," said Lewis, "that when this capricious and violent current sets against its banks, which are usually covered with heavy timber, it quickly undermines them, sometimes to the depth of forty or fifty paces, and several miles in length. The banks being unable to support themeslves longer, tumble into the river with tremendous force, destroying everything within their reach. The timber thus precipitated into the water with large masses of earth about their roots are seen drifting with the stream, their points above the water, while the roots more heavy, are dragged along the bottom until they become firmly fixed in the quicksands, which form the bed of the river, where they remain for many years, forming an irregular tho' dangerous *cheveaux de frise* to oppose the navigator." A year later, Lewis was still amazed that the boats had not been buried by one of these landslides that were eternally dropping into the river with a muffled roar. "We have had many hairbreadth escapes from them but Providence seems to have ordered it that we have as yet sustained no loss in consequence of them."

Sunken trees and half-submerged logs—"sawyers," or "planters," rivermen called them—presented another peril. The river's turbid water, filled with suspended sand and soil, made it hard "to discover any obstruction even to the depth of a single inch." "Drifts," or *embarras*, as the French called them—masses of driftwood—often lodged at the point of an island and were difficult to pass and when dislodged swept downstream like an avalanche. Worst of all were the rolling sandbars, constantly agitated by the racing river. The water ran over them "with such violence that if your vessel happens to touch the sand, or is by any accident turned sidewise to the current, it is driven on the bar and overset in an instant, generally destroyed, and always attended with the loss of the cargo."

On May 24, the barge hit a sandbar. Cruzatte, guiding up the left or larboard bank as the nautical-minded Clark called it, saw the bank start to crumble. Several of the crew were ashore helping the oarsmen inch the boat upstream by rope. Cruzatte signalled the helmsman to head for the starboard bank, but in mid-river the

Eastern woodrat, engraving by Charles A. Lesueur
LIBRARY, THE ACADEMY OF NATURAL SCIENCES OF PHILADELPHIA

barge thudded against the hidden bar. "The swiftness of the current wheeled the boat, broke our tow rope, and was nearly oversetting the boat. All hands jumped out on the upper side and bore on that side until the sand washed from under the boat and wheeled on the next bank. She wheeled and lodged on the bank below as often as three times before we got her in deep water. By the time she wheeled a third time, [we] got a rope fast to her stern and by the means of swimmers [she] was carried to shore."

The party quickly settled into a routine largely drawn from the captains' military experience. All rose with the sun. In the early days they ate first before taking to the river, but later they struck camp on rising and traveled until around nine o'clock before stopping for breakfast. Dinner came any time between noon and two o'clock when a good site appeared. After a rest whose length depended on how hard the morning's labor had been, they went back to the river until sunset. Whenever the party camped by a large stream flowing into the Missouri, the captains spent the evening fixing its geographical location by the stars. Lewis had purchased the best chronometer available in Philadelphia and one of the sergeants had the duty of winding it each day at noon.

Several times during the trip the instrument, crucial to accurate observations, proved balky and stopped dead. Even so, scholars who have checked Lewis' calculations have found them "remarkably accurate . . . throughout."

The hunters flushed little game while the boats remained within range of the river settlements, and so in the early days on the water the party dined off its larder. They breakfasted on hominy—corn that had been soaked in lye water until the hard husks had peeled off—or grits—lyed corn ground in the steel mill nailed to the barge's gunwale. Clark would have liked coffee for an eye-opener, but they carried only fifty pounds of roasted beans, barely enough for special occasions. (Coffee was high on the list two years later when the party neared civilization on the return trip and Clark sent a man ahead to a British trading post to barter for a few provisions.) The menu offered salt pork as the entrée for dinner, sometimes topped off with suet dumplings, made with flour mixed with fat and water and then boiled. Supper brought more pork and perhaps some parched corn, a favorite staple. The corn was fried in grease until slightly burned, then dried over an open fire. The men munched it like popcorn or peanuts and it went well with the ration of whisky that came in the evening.

This menu varied only slightly during the first month, an anxious one for the captains as they saw the larder diminish. The hunters gleaned little from the land. They shot seventy deer, about a dozen bear, and little else—a slim haul that fed the crew for only two and a half weeks.

The hunters rode ahead of the boats. They packed whatever they shot to the river and hung it from a tree—high enough to be out of reach of wolves but in a spot where the boats coming up could see it. The "best pieces"—the hams and tenderloins of a deer's haunch, the hump and tongue of a buffalo, the tail and tongue of a beaver—were eaten first. But nothing was wasted. Bones were cracked for the marrow within them. Hides were converted into robes or moccasins or clothing. The rendered fat would reappear as soup stock, mosquito repellent, soap, candles—its uses were endless.

The men never hesitated to experiment with whatever the land offered. Less than a week out of Saint Charles they tried a species of cress found in the river bottoms and of it made "a very pleasant wholesome salad." A kind of kale, new to everyone, they "boiled green and found it healthy and pleasant." They adapted easily to each new geographical world they moved into and in time were relishing what once would have never crossed their lips—the broiled testicles of a beaver, the toasted entrails of a buffalo stuffed with chopped meat, the haunch of an Indian dog. As tastes changed, so, too, did clothing. First went the army shoes, which weighed like lead when slogging along river bottoms or lifting boats over bars. From parties coming down after a winter on the Missouri, they bought moccasins and buckskins. The *engagés* later taught the men how to make their clothing from deer hides. But wilderness ways intruded only so far on army routine. The men continued to shave regularly and probably cut one another's hair as it grew uncomfortably long. The captains consulted the crew where decisions were crucial but they did not tolerate familiarity. They, with Drouillard, who had special status as interpreter, messed apart; York cooked for them.

The captains issued all orders jointly but each informally allotted certain areas of responsibility to himself. Lewis, as the scientist, spent most of his days ashore studying the flora and fauna of the country. Clark, as meteorologist, each day at dawn and 4 P.M. meticulously recorded the temperature (until the last thermometer was broken), the wind direction, sky covering, and general weather. As cartographer, he chalked on a piece of slate every twist and bend in the river, its course and width, the streams that entered it, the distances logged between prominent points, and later he transferred this information to a notebook. As an experienced riverman, he also ran the barge, or batteaux as he called it, and no doubt it was he who worked out the daily routine of its operation in the orders issued early during the shakedown.

26 May 1804

The post and duties of the sergeants shall be as follows, viz.—when the batteaux is under way, one sergeant shall be stationed at the helm, one in the center on the rear of the starboard locker, and one at the bow. The sergeant at the helm shall steer the boat and see that the baggage on the quarterdeck is properly arranged and stowed away in the most advantageous manner; see that no cooking utensils or loose lumber of any kind is left on the deck to obstruct the passage between the berths—he will also attend to the compass when necessary.

The sergeant at the center will command the guard, manage the sails, see that the men at the oars do their duty; that they come on board at a proper season in the morning, and that the boat gets underway in due time. He will keep a good lookout for the mouths of all rivers, creeks, islands, and other remarkable places and shall immediately report the same to the commanding officers. He will attend to the issues of spirituous liquors. He shall regulate the halting of the batteaux through the day to give the men refreshments, and will also regulate the time of her departure, taking care that not more time than is necessary shall be expended at each halt. It shall be his duty also to post a sentinel on the bank near the boat whenever we come to and halt in the course of the day. At the same time he will (accompanied by two of his guard) reconnoiter the forest around the place of landing to the distance of at least one hundred paces. When we come to for the purpose of encamping at night, the sergeant of the guard shall post two sentinels immediately on our landing, one of whom shall be posted near the boat and the other at a convenient distance in the rear of the encampment. At night the sergeant must be always present with his guard, and he is positively forbidden to suffer any man of his guard to absent himself on any pretext whatever. He will at each relief through the night, accompanied by the two men last off their posts, reconnoiter in every direction around the camp to the distance of at least one hundred and fifty paces, and also examine the situation of the boats and pirogues and see that they lie safe and free from the bank.

It shall be the duty of the sergeant at the bow to keep a good look out for all danger which may approach, either of the enemy or obstructions which may present themselves to the passage of the boat. Of the first he will notify the sergeant at the center, who will communicate the information to the commanding officers, and of the second or obstructions to the boat he will notify the sergeant at the helm. He will also report to the commanding officers through the sergeant at the center all pirogues, boats, canoes, or other craft which he may discover in the river, and all hunting camps or parties of Indians in view of which we may pass. He will at all times be provided with a setting pole and assist the bowman in poling and managing the bow of the boat. It will be his duty also to give and answer all signals which may hereafter be established for the government of the pirogues and parties on shore.

The sergeants will on each morning before our departure relieve each other in the following manner, viz.—The sergeants at the helm will parade the new guard, relieve the sergeant and the old guard, and occupy the middle station in the boat. The sergeant of the old guard will occupy the station at the bow and the sergeant who had been stationed in the preceding day at the bow will place himself at the helm.

The sergeants in addition to those duties are directed each to keep a separate journal from day to day of all passing occurrences and such other observations on the country, etc., as shall appear to them worthy of notice.

The sergeants are relieved and exempt from all labor of making fires, pitching tents, or cooking and will direct and make the men of their several messes perform an equal proportion of those duties.

The guard shall hereafter consist of one sergeant and six privates and engagés.

Patroon Deschamps, Corporal Warfington, and George Drouillard are exempt from guard duty. The two former will attend particularly to their pirogues at all times and see that their lading is in good order, and that the same is kept perfectly free from rain or other moisture. The latter will perform certain duties on shore which will be assigned him from time to time. All other soldiers and engaged men of whatever description must perform their regular tour of guard duty.

All details for guard or other duty will be made in the evening when we encamp, and the duty to be performed will be entered on by the individuals so warned the next morning. Provision for one day will be issued to the party on each evening after we have encamped. The same will be cooked on that evening by the several messes and a proportion of it reserved for the next day as no cooking will be allowed in the day while on the march.

Sergeant Ordway will continue to issue the provisions and make the details for guard or other duty.

The day after tomorrow lyed corn and grease will be issued to the party. The next day pork and flour, and the day following Indian meal and pork. And in conformity to that routine provisions will continue to be issued to the party until further orders. Should any of the messes prefer Indian meal to flour they may receive it accordingly. No pork is to be issued when we have fresh meat on hand.

Labiche and Cruzatte will man the larboard bow oar alternately, and the one not engaged at the oar will attend as the bowman, and when the attention of both these persons is necessary at the bow their oar is to be manned by any idle hand on board.

MERIWETHER LEWIS, CAPTAIN

WILLIAM CLARK, CAPTAIN

Chapter 8

Flora and Fauna

The river remained as it had been and would be to the end—difficult. Dawn rarely gave much to cheer about for men who had to row and pole and pull upstream inch by inch some twenty tons of goods against a swift current strewn with hazards. Yet good humor prevailed and the nights more often than not ended with singing and dancing. A few incidents stood out in the long haul up to the Mandan villages. Sergeant Floyd died from a burst appendix. (He would have died even if attended by the best physicians of the day, for the illness was then inoperable.) He was buried, "much lamented," on the crest of a bluff and near a stream the party named Floyd's River. The party almost lost Shannon, too. Thinking the boats ahead of him when they were behind, he marched upstream for two weeks and was close to starvation when finally found. There were serious infractions of discipline. Willard fell asleep on guard duty, and although he pleaded guilty only "of lying down," his peers ordered he receive one hundred lashes for a dereliction that could have led "to the probable destruction of the party" now that it was crossing through enemy country. Reed and one of the engagés, La Liberte, deserted. La Liberte vanished for good, but Reed was caught. Newman made "criminal and mutinous expressions" against Lewis. After running the gauntlet both men were drummed out of the expedition; they would remain on as working hands until able to return with the barge from the Mandan villages.

Except for Floyd's death, these incidents faded into the background for the party as a whole as the boats each day edged deeper into a strange new world. On July 4, the expedition celebrated with an extra dram of ardent spirits, and that may help account for Clark's exuberance as he described the land they were moving through.

The plains of this country are covered with a leek green grass, well calculated for the sweetest and most nourishing hay—interspersed with copses of trees, spreading their lofty branches over pools, springs, or brooks of fine water. Groups of shrubs covered with the most delicious fruit is to be seen in every direction, and nature appears to have exerted herself to beautify the scenery by the variety of flowers, delicately and highly flavored, raised above the grass, which strikes and perfumes the sensations and amuses the mind, throws it into conjecturing the cause of so magnificent a scenery . . . in a country situated far removed from the civilized world to be enjoyed by nothing but the buffalo, elk, deer, and bear in which it abounds and . . . savage Indians.

Never before had Clark so exposed his feelings on paper. He omitted this passage when copying out the day's entry from the rough journal. (Clark constantly had to censor himself. A few days later he carved his name and the date on an Indian grave marker. Out, too, went that trivial incident in the second draft.) But his exuberance could not be suppressed, especially when below the Platte River the party moved into another new but equally beautiful world. After hiking one morning through a strip of cottonwoods that lined the river, he "came suddenly into an open and boundless prairie. I say boundless because I could not see the end of the plain in any direction." The prairie was covered with a rich growth of "grass from five to eight feet high, interspersed with copses of hazel, plums, currants (like those of the United States), raspberries, and grapes of different kinds."

Above the Platte one of the men killed "an animal called by the French brarow [blaireau or badger as English traders named it]" because it burrowed for its food. None of the Americans had seen anything like it. Its legs were short, "just sufficient to raise his body above the ground." It had the shape and size of a beaver, the mouth and ears of a dog, the tail and hair of a ground hog. The captains had its skin preserved to send back to President Jefferson as the expedition's first contribution to zoology. No one then knew, not even the usually knowledgeable President, that the badger had been described for science twenty-six years earlier from a specimen found in Canada.

A few days later, on August 5, came two real finds when a snake and a tern were killed. Both were known to French members of the party but not to the Americans or to science. The snake was "vulgarly called the cow or bull snake from a bellowing noise which it is said sometimes to make resembling that animal. . . ." The tern, which Lewis had observed along the river for several days before bagging one, "lives on small fish, worms, and bugs which it takes on the verge of the water. It is seldom seen to light on trees and quite as seldom do they light in the water and swim, tho' the foot would indicate that they did, its being webbed." In his precise description he noted that "the wings when folded lap like that of the swallow and extend at least an inch and a half beyond the tail. This bird is very noisy when flying, which it does extremely swift. The motion of the wing is much like that of kill-dee. It has two notes, one like the squawking of a small pig only on rather a higher key, and the other kit-tee-kit-tee as near as letters can express the sound."

*Prairie apple, discovered June
or July, 1804, hand-colored
engraving by W. Hooker*
LIBRARY, THE ACADEMY OF NATURAL
SCIENCES OF PHILADELPHIA

The first plant Lewis preserved that would turn out to be new
to science was a showy flower that began to be abundant at the
mouth of the Platte—the pink cleone. On the stretch of the river
between the Platte and the Mandan villages, where Lewis began
his serious collecting, he preserved thirty-eight plants, nineteen of
which were then unknown to botany. This was not bad for someone who had read little in the field and of whom Jefferson said
that in zoology he "is more skilled than in botany." Some of these
finds may have been thanks to Clark, who knew more natural history than he has been given credit for. It was Clark, for example,
who first noted in his journal the buffaloberry—"a berry resembling
a currant except double the size and grows on a bush like a privet
and the size of a damsen, deliciously flavored and makes delightful

tarts"—and perhaps persuaded Lewis to preserve a specimen, which he did some time later. The buffaloberry turned out to be new to science.

Above the Platte, the flora and fauna changed and so did the party's diet, for on August 23 the first buffalo was shot. Lewis took eleven men out to help butcher the beast and bring in the carcass, which weighed somewhere between a thousand and fifteen hundred pounds. The rest of the day belonged to the experienced *engagés*. They knew how to skin the beast to preserve the hide for a robe. They knew the best pieces for eating—the tongue, the hump, the fleece, which was the flesh between the spine and ribs covered with fat, the side ribs and the belly fat—and how to cook them. The hump tasted best when boiled and the other pieces when roasted on a stick over the camp fire. The *engagés* liked to gorge on the fat, and if the party followed their lead here everyone suffered the next few days from *le mal de vache*, a mild dysentery that lasted until the body adjusted to the fatty diet. Oddly, none of the journals remarked on this first feast of "indescribably rich, tender, fiberless, and gamey beef, . . . the greatest meat man has ever fed on."

On September 4, the expedition reached the Niobrara River, gateway to another strange new world—the High Plains within which they would live until they reached the foothills of the Rocky Mountains nearly a year later. The tall, lush grass below had been supplanted by a short, tough covering. The deer and elk and buffalo thrived on it, for the herds, of modest size below, now began to be immense, numbering in the hundreds, sometimes even the thousands. The air was pure and dry and the clear sky seldom clouded over, for this was a semi-arid region rarely drenched with rain. The flora and fauna changed as abruptly as the landscape. In the next two weeks Lewis preserved fifteen plants he thought might be new to science; eight of them were. During the same period the party met with six mammals and two birds none of which had ever been seen before; all turned out to be indigenous to the High Plains and new to science.

The first new animal to turn up came three days past the Niobrara when Lewis and Clark "discovered a village of small animals that burrow in the ground." The *engagés* had prepared the captains for the small beasts, which they called "les petits chiens." For some reason the Voyage of Discovery preferred to call them "burrowing" or "barking" squirrels. True, they burrowed, they barked, and except for their short tails they looked like squirrels, but later travelers followed the French lead and gave them the name that stuck—prairie dogs. They were gregarious and lived in villages that often approached the size of cities. (Clark a few days later came upon one that he estimated was two-thirds of a mile long and nearly a half mile wide.)

Before them the captains saw a scene changeless through history, one perfectly described by a later prairie voyager. "Approaching a 'village,' the little dogs may be observed frisking about the 'streets'—passing from dwelling to dwelling apparently on visits—sometimes a few clustered together as though in council—here

*Black-tailed prairie dog, discovered September 7, 1805,
engraving by J.J. Barralet*
LIBRARY, THE ACADEMY OF NATURAL SCIENCES OF PHILADELPHIA

feeding upon the tender herbage—there cleaning their 'houses,' or brushing the little hillock about the door—yet all quiet. Upon seeing a stranger, however, each streaks to its home, but is apt to stop at the entrance, and spread the general alarm by a succession of shrill yelps, usually sitting erect. Yet at the report of a gun or the too near approach of the visitor, they dart down and are seen no more till the cause of alarm seems to have disappeared."

Moments after the captains came in view, the lively village became dead quiet. Orders went back for the floating caravan to come ashore and for all the crew to join in capturing one of the small beasts. First they tried to dig to the bottom of one of the burrows, but "after digging six feet found by running a pole down that we were not halfway to his lodge." Now and then a "squirrel" peeped from his hole and made a taunting "whistling noise" at the sweating crew. The decision to flush—literally—one of the animals out led to hauling kettle after kettle of river water up to the village. "We poured into one of the holes five barrels of water without filling it," but finally one of the "squirrels" came floating out. The party had spent a good part of the day to win the tiny but living trophy.

The prairie dog amused the crew. The antelope and jack rabbit fascinated them. The French called the antelope a wild goat or cabra, the Spanish word for goat. It looked like a cross between a deer and a goat, it tasted somewhat like goat, but Lewis held that "he is more like the antelope or gazelle of Africa than any other species of goat"; because of Lewis' insistence, the American pronghorn has forever after been forced to travel under a false name. Its speed was amazing. It did not bound across the landscape like a deer but skimmed the ground "as though upon skates." When aroused, their swiftness made it impossible to get a bead on them, but the men soon found them easy to kill because they were "very inquisitive usually to learn what we are as we pass, and frequently accompanying us at no great distance for miles, frequently halting and giving a loud whistle through their nostrils."

September 14, the day Clark killed the first antelope, Shields

brought in a new species of hare. Its long ears, which resembled those of a jackass and led to the name jack rabbit, intrigued Lewis. "The ears are placed at the upper part of the head and very near to each other; the ears are very flexible. The animal moves them with great ease and quickness and can contract and fold them on his back or dilate them at pleasure." Later he measured the hare's leap at twenty-one feet, and he began to wonder if the antelope was after all the fleetest beast on the prairie. "These hares," he said, "appear to run with more ease and to bound with greater agility than any animal I ever saw." The great day for American zoology ended with both "the goat and rabbit stuffed" for shipping to the President.

On September 16, Lewis killed a bird whose unusual beauty lay hidden behind a pedestrian name—magpie. Buried within Lewis' long, typically precise yet vivid description of the bird is a passage the length of a paragraph devoted just to the tail feathers:

Pronghorn, discovered September 14, 1805,
engraving by Alexander Lawson
LIBRARY, THE ACADEMY OF NATURAL SCIENCES OF PHILADELPHIA

Black-billed Magpie, *discovered September 16, 1804,*
watercolor by Titian Peale

The plumage of the tail consists of twelve feathers of equal lengths
by pairs. Those in the center are the longest and the others on
each side diminishing about an inch each pair. The underside of
the feathers is a pale black, the upper side is a dark bluish green
and which like the outer part of the wings is changeable as it
reflects different portions of light. Towards the extremity of these
feathers they become of an orange green, then shaded pass to a
reddish indigo blue, and again at the extremity assume the pre-
dominant color of changeable green. The tints of these feathers are
very similar and equally beautiful and rich as the tints of blue and
green of the peacock. It is a most beautiful bird.

Technically the bird was not new to science. It was well known
in Europe. No one, however, had dreamt until now that it also
existed in North America. And having never seen a specimen be-

fore, he naturally but mistakenly assumed that the American species differed from the European one.

On September 17, the expedition gave science another new animal when Colter killed "a curious kind of deer." Clark's usual succinct report described it as "of a dark gray color, more so than common, hair long and fine, the ears large and long." It had "a tuft of black hair about the end" and jumped, unlike eastern deer, "like a goat or sheep." The *engagés* called it the black-tailed deer, but Lewis eight months later reported that the American crew had "adapted the appelation of the mule deer, which I think much more appropriate," and thus the animal has since been known.

On September 18, Clark killed an animal that had pestered the party for a month and a half—barking "like a large fierce dog" nightly, just beyond the rim of the camp fires. Clark called it a prairie wolf but the *engagés* may have known and passed along the Spanish name—coyote. It was as the crew found out in time smaller than a dog, the color of a wolf, twice as rapacious as either animal yet the parasite, the jackal, of the prairies, too cowardly to forage for its food except on the remains of what other animals brought down. The gray wolf, which Clark the same day distinguished as a species separate from the wolf he had known back east, was not a much more meritorious animal. It traipsed behind buffalo or elk herds waiting to cut off a weak calf or faltering cow, then, with a victim in sight, it would flash in to cut a hamstring or gnaw a leg muscle until the beast had been immobilized.

The number and variety of animals previously unknown to the crew above the Niobrara was a daily miracle. "I walked on shore, saw goats, elk, buffalo, black-tailed deer, and the common deer," Clark wrote on the day he killed the first coyote. He also saw that day: "porcupine, rabbits, and barking squirrels in this quarter"; he added as an afterthought, "plums and grapes."

Chapter 9

"The Pirates of the Missouri"

Later, in their report to Jefferson on the Indians met on the way up to the Mandan villages, Lewis and Clark said of the Teton Sioux: "These are the vilest miscreants of the savage race and must ever remain the pirates of the Missouri until such measures are pursued by our government as will make them feel a dependence on its will for their supply of merchandise. . . . The tameness with which the traders of the Missouri have heretofore submitted to their rapacity has tended not a little to inspire them with contempt for the white persons who visit them through that channel."

The party met their first Teton Sioux on September 23. The day began well. A soft breeze from the southeast allowed sails to be set. The river stretched ahead in an almost straight line, pocked with sandbars but wide enough to maneuver around them. Only herds of grazing buffalo blotted the endless sea of grass that spread away from the river. In mid-morning a screen of smoke rose off to the south. Someone had set fire to the prairie to warn Indians upstream that strangers approached. The party camped late in the afternoon in a copse of trees on the east side of the river. Soon afterward three Sioux boys swam over. They said two villages of Teton Sioux lay a short distance upstream, one of eighty lodges, one of sixty lodges. Yes, they had set the prairie on fire "to let those camps know of our approach." The boys swam away with two twists of tobacco for their chiefs.

Dawn brought another fair day and another good sailing breeze from the southeast. Every man sat with rifle handy. The captains unpacked their formal uniforms. Early in the day the party came to the mouth of the Bad River where the first of the Sioux villages lay. They anchored on a sandbar and Clark went ashore to arrange a grand council. That night two-thirds of the crew slept on board the barge, and the remainder stood guard on the sandbar.

The next morning preparations began for a performance in which, after three dress rehearsals with friendly tribes downstream, everyone had his lines down pat. The sandbar served as the stage. The barge's mast was fixed there to serve as a flag pole. The barge's awning, stretched flat on poles, gave shade for the ceremony. The men dressed in their parade uniforms. Mid-morning saw the mouth of the Bad River blackened with Indians, "who came flocking in from both sides." An hour later the grand chief, Black Buffalo, arrived in full regalia. With him came two lesser chiefs, Buffalo Medicine and Partisan. (Earlier, a trader the party had met coming downstream warned to watch out for Partisan whom he called the worst villain on the river.) They brought with them as a present a great pile of buffalo meat that gave off a pungent odor. The Americans thought they had been insulted, given something about to be thrown away. They did not then know that the Plains Indians considered rank meat delicious.

Nor did the Indians—"rather ugly and ill-made, their legs and arms being too small, their cheekbones high, and their eyes projecting"—make a good impression. They shaved their heads bare, except for a long tuft worn in a plait. Face and body were painted with what seemed a blend of grease and coal dust. Over the shoulders they wore buffalo robes "laced with porcupine quills loosely fixed so as to make a jingling noise when in motion." Close by the chiefs stood men dressed differently from the rest of the tribe. Each wore "two or three raven skins so fixed on the small of the back in such a way that the tails stick horizontally off from the body, fixed to the girdle; and on his forehead a raven skin split in two, tied around his head with the beak sticking out from his forehead." These were the chiefs' "soldiers," as Clark called them, chosen to keep peace in the tribe, their authority limited only by their chiefs' wills. "They generally accompany the chief and if ordered by him to do any duty however dangerous it is a point of honor for the soldier to die rather than desist or refuse to obey."

At noon the American colors were raised. The three chiefs settled under the awning with thirty of their warriors and soldiers, and after "smoking agreeable to the usual custom," Lewis read the opening speech. It was a long one: "expressive of our journey, the wishes of our government, some advice to them and direction how they were to conduct themselves." It went badly. Cruzatte had difficulty translating, "and therefore," wrote Lewis, "we curtailed our harangue." Presents were passed out—to the grand chief an American flag, a medal of Jefferson, a laced uniform with a cocked hat and feather; to the lesser chiefs smaller medals, a blanket, leggings, garters, some tobacco, and knives. Partisan glowered over his small haul.

While the tribe looked on from the river bank the chiefs, each accompanied by a soldier, were rowed out to the barge. There the captains entertained them with the mysteries of the compass, the telescope, the magnet, and the airgun, all of which were "incomprehensible to them," especially the air gun. "They cannot comprehend its shooting so often and without powder, and think that it is great medicine which comprehends everything that is to them incomprehensible." After the show ended, half a wine glass of whisky was passed out to each visitor. Each downed it quickly and asked for more. 'No more,' came the word. "They took up an empty bottle, smelt it, and made many simple gestures, and soon began to be troublesome." One chief said the expedition "must stop with them or leave one of the pirogues with them, as that was what they expected." The captains said they "did not wish to be detained any longer." The chiefs must go ashore, the boats would move upstream. Partisan pretended to be drunk and reeled about the deck. The crew with difficulty piled the Indians into the pirogue and, with Clark aboard, rowed to the sandbar. Instantly, as the boat touched ground, an Indian soldier threw his arms about the mast. Clark knew that "no force except the command of his chief would have induced him to release his hold."

Clark turned to the chiefs and said, "we are not squaws, but warriors." Partisan said that he, too, had warriors. Then he became "exceedingly insolent, both in words and gestures to me [Clark], declaring I should not go off, saying he had not received presents sufficient from us," that his men "would follow us and take the whole of us by degrees." Clark became "warm, and spoke in very positive tones." Partisan raged on. Clark drew his sword. The tier of warriors behind the chiefs drew arrows from their quivers and bent their bows. Lewis on the barge ordered every man to his arms. Sixteen musket balls were poured into the swivel cannon. Blunderbusses were loaded with buckshot and trained on shore. Twelve men jumped into the second pirogue and rowed toward the sandbar.

The grand chief now stepped forward. He waved away the soldier hugging the mast of the first pirogue and another gripping the landing line. He took the line in his own hands. He asked if the tribe's women and children could visit the barge, "as they never saw such a one." Clark refused. The caravan was moving upstream, if only to let the warriors know that Clark could not be stopped. The chief said he knew the captains were not merchants and had no goods to trade but was sorry to have them leave so soon. He then dropped the landing line and moved back to where the other chiefs stood watching, flanked by their warriors. "All this time the Indians were pointing their arrows blank" at Clark. He stepped up and offered his hand. The grand chief ignored it. Clark returned to the pirogue and ordered the men to shove off. When the oars hit water, the first and third chiefs—Partisan still sulked—and two of their soldiers waded into the river and begged to spend the night on the barge. Clark knew when to bristle and when to forget an insult. Once all were back on the barge, the expedition moved out. It traveled to an island a mile upstream, far enough to make the point that the decision when to move lay with the Americans, not the Indians. "I call this Bad Humored Island," Clark said.

The party arose after a restless, watchful night to find the shore again thick with Indians. The boats got underway at once, despite pleas from the chiefs for a show of friendship. Lay over for a day, they begged, and let the tribe honor the white men with a banquet and dance. The captains relented. "Our conduct yesterday seemed to have inspired the Indians with fear of us, and as we were desirous of cultivating their acquaintance we complied with their wish."

The banquet came in the late afternoon. Clark, in dress uniform, went ashore first. Upon landing, the natives placed him on "an elegant painted buffalo robe" and in grand style he was "taken to the village by six men and was not permitted to touch the ground until I was put down in the grand council house on a white dressed robe." The commodious council house held some seventy Indians, who sat in a large semi-circle. Clark's bearers placed him between two chiefs. Before him lay a pipe of peace raised on crotched sticks; beneath the pipe lay a scattering of swansdown. Earlier, Spanish representatives had told the tribe it owed allegiance to Spain; yesterday the captains had said the United States was their sovereign. The chiefs had resolved the confusion by flanking the pipe of peace with the flag of each nation. In front of the flags blazed a large fire in which dinner was cooking. Nearby lay a mound of some four hundred pounds of buffalo meat. The Indians had learned since yesterday that the Americans did not like rank meat. Clark judged this offering of fresh cuts excellent.

Soon after Clark had been ceremoniously lowered into place, in came Lewis elevated on a robe. An old man of the tribe now rose and "As far as we could learn [he] spoke approving what we had done." The grand chief, after a few words to the same purpose, solemnly took up the pipe of peace, pointed it to the heavens, to the four corners of the earth, moved to the fire and "took in one hand some of the most delicate parts of the dog, which was prepared for the feast and made a sacrifice to the flag," then presented to the guests the stem of the pipe to smoke.

The menu consisted of broiled dog, pemmican, and "ground potato" (a wild root commonly called "prairie turnip" or "prairie apple"). Clark liked the pemmican and ground potato but not the dog. Lewis found the ground potato tasteless but recalling his days in the President's mansion wrote, "our epicures would admire this root very much; it would serve them in their ragouts and gravies instead of truffles morella." He liked the dog, and so did the men, who had been ushered into the banquet with less elegance than their captains. The meal was served on wooden platters and eaten with the curved horn of a mountain sheep that held about two quarts in the scoop.

After dinner, everyone smoked until dark. The remains of the feast were cleared away and around a great bonfire a dance began. First came the warriors dressed for the occasion with skunk pelts tied to the heels of their moccasins; the pelts trailed in the dust as the men shuffled along. Several of the men rattled tambourines adorned with deer and antelope hoofs. "Having arranged themselves in two columns, one on each side of the fire, as soon as the music began they danced towards each other till they met in the center, when the rattles were shaken, and they all shouted and returned to their places. They have no step, but shuffle along the ground; nor does the music appear to be anything more than a confusion of noises, distinguished only by hard or gentle blows upon the buffalo skins; the song is perfectly extemporaneous." Occasionally, some of the men would break from the shuffle and jump

Dog Dance of the Plains Indian,
aquatint of watercolor by Karl Bodmer

up and down, adding whoops and yells to the musical accompaniment. And every now and then a warrior would step from his line and come forward to recite "in a short or low guttural tone some little story or incident, which is either martial or ludicrous; or, as was the case this evening, voluptuous and indecent; this is taken up by the orchestra and the dancers, who repeat it in a high strain and dance to it."

The women, who danced apart from the men, now came forth, decorated with the "trophies of war of their fathers, husbands, and relations, and 'danced the war dance, which they did with great cheerfulness." They were still dancing with cheerfulness at midnight when the captains, who had slept little the night before, "informed the chief we intended to return on board." ("They offered us women, which we did not accept.") Again the chiefs spent the night aboard the barge, and again the commanders had "a bad night's sleep."

At dawn the expedition rose to a river blanketed with Indians. The sight made the party feel like the cast in a traveling side-show. The chiefs said that "a great part of their nation had not arrived and would arrive tonight and requested us to delay one day longer that they might see us." The Teton Sioux for years had intimidated traders coming upstream from Saint Louis; their commercial ties were with the British traders from Canada. The time would be well spent if their allegiance could be swung to the Great Father in Washington. The captains agreed to lay over one more day.

They spent the day making their presence felt, moving cautiously but calmly through the village, always with a guard of their own men. The tribe's lodges were like nothing the captains had seen. They housed ten people comfortably. From a distance they looked like huge sugar loaves. "They are built round with poles about fifteen or twenty feet high, covered with white skins; these lodges may be taken to pieces, packed up, and carried with the nation wherever they go, by dogs, which bear great burdens." From a group of Omaha prisoners they came upon—"a wretched and dejected looking people"—Cruzatte learned that the Sioux had vowed we were "to be stopped" from moving upstream.

Evening brought another banquet, another dance, but no visitors from the village upstream. The captains, with two sleepless nights behind them, ended the festivities early. The chiefs again asked to spend the night aboard the barge. While Lewis during the ferrying stayed on shore with his bodyguard alert, Clark headed out with Partisan and another chief to the barge. An inexperienced man at the steering sweep sent the boat too far upriver. The current swung her full force against the bow of the barge, snapping the anchor cable. Clark shouted to those on board that the barge was adrift. "My peremptory order to the men and the bustle of their getting to their oars alarmed the chiefs. . . . The chiefs hallowed and alarmed the camp or town, informing them that the Mahars was about attacking us." Instantly, the grand chief materialized on shore with warriors armed for action. Within minutes the crew had the barge under control and tied to shore. Something like calm followed. The swift appearance of the armed Indians convinced the captains the Sioux meant to anihilate the expedition given the chance. Half the crew stood sentry duty ashore the rest of the night. "No sleep," wrote Clark.

With dawn the party started searching for the barge's lost anchor. They poked the bottom of the river with boat hooks and poles. That failing, they "took a cord and put sinks to the middle and took each end to the two pirogues and dragged the river diligently a long time. . . ." Finally, at ten o'clock, Clark called a halt, the men breakfasted, then turned to the oars. The chiefs protested. They said the party could stay with the Sioux or return unmolested to Saint Louis, but "could not go up the Missouri any farther." As they spoke, several warriors sat by the barge's landing line and some two hundred Indians lined the bank, armed with guns and spears and bows with iron-tipped arrows. Clark surveyed the scene cooly, then called for the sail to be hoisted and his men to the oars. He ordered a man ashore to untie the landing line; the warriors snapped it from him "and tied it faster than before." Clark lost his temper and directed the grand chief off the barge. "We are sorry to have you go," the chief said. "But if you will give us one carrot of tobacco we will be willing for you to go on and will not try to stop you." Clark threw a packet of tobacco at the chief, picked up a blunderbuss, and said: "You have told us you are a great man—have influence—take this tobacco and show us you have influence by taking the rope from your men and letting us go without coming to hostilities." The chief passed the tobacco to the warriors, jerked the line from them and passed it to the bowman on the barge. Later, from another chief, the captains learned the trouble had been the work of Partisan, "a double-spoken man." Clark, however, blamed all the chiefs and their people. Although a forgiving man, he never forgave the Teton Sioux. When, on the return trip, they appeared again to threaten his party, he told them "to keep away from the river or we should kill everyone of them, etc., etc." He also told them that "they had been deef to our councils and ill-treated us as we ascended this river two years past, that they had abused the whites who had visited them since. I believed them to be a bad people."

An hour and a half after the boats moved upstream again the captains stopped to make a new anchor of stones and to refresh everyone with a dram of whisky. They camped early on a sandbar in the middle of the river. "Determined to sleep tonight if possible," said Clark. "I am very unwell, I think for want of sleep."

Chapter 10

Fort Mandan

The expedition spent the winter of 1804–1805 on the edge of an Indian metropolis of three loosely joined tribes—the Mandan, Minitari, and Amahami—whose 4,400 souls comprised the largest concentration of Indians on the entire Missouri. The population was dispersed through five villages, each surrounded by sturdy earthen walls behind which clustered mound-like lodges, each large enough to house several families, their horses and dogs.

Despite the arctic-like winter, the half year respite from the river passed pleasantly. The crew lived fairly comfortably in the triangular-shaped Fort Mandan which they built a few miles below the Indian villages. They did not lack for female companionship. French and British traders who commuted from Canadian posts, though treated with cool courtesy, gave relief from the constant presence of the Indians. Game was less plentiful than expected but the natives, especially the Mandans, took up the slack with contributions from their own larder.

Interior of the Hut of a Mandan Chief,
aquatint of watercolor by Karl Bodmer
RARE BOOK DIVISION, THE NEW YORK PUBLIC LIBRARY,
ASTOR, LENOX AND TILDEN FOUNDATIONS

The weeks usually passed uneventfully. One night an Indian had to be restrained from killing his wife, who had slept with Ordway. Pryor threw out his shoulder and it took four tortuous trials before the men could twist it back in place. York returned one afternoon from a trip on the prairies with his feet frost-bitten "and his p————s a little." Christmas was spent with much dancing interspersed with several rations of rum and brandy. On New Year's Day sixteen of the men danced for one of the villages that had reacted sullenly to the expedition's presence. York, whose blackness intrigued the Indians—one chief tried to rub off his "black paint" with moistened fingers—was the hit of the show. His dance "amused the crowd very much, and somewhat astonished them that so large a man should be active, etc., etc." Through the rest of the winter so little occurred worth reporting that the phrase "nothing remarkable happened today" appeared regularly in the journals.

The captains, however, did not want for things to do. From the day they arrived among the villages their thoughts and energy centered on the cargo they would send back to the President and the War Department in the spring of 1805. The contents of that shipment would be the most remarkable ever received by any government whose citizens had explored the land west of the Mississippi. Spain, France, and Great Britain had sent able, perceptive men into the region, but their reports had been classified as secret and thus did little to sweep away for the public the mists that shrouded that vast territory. Also, their reports had been generally shaped to answer a single question—where in the broad expanses of the West were the spots that offered quick, rich profits to those who dared to penetrate them? Lewis and Clark, under the constant influence of Jefferson's instructions, had looked at the land they passed through from a variety of angles—as geographers, ethnologists, mineralogists, zoologists, botanists, agronomists, and ornithologists. They, like others before them, studied the Indians to learn how to control them but also simply to understand them and their way of life. They sifted through the flora and fauna for specimens that would be new to science. As they looked at the land, they saw beyond the immediate and immense profit in furs and peltry waiting to be harvested and studied its value for Americans east of the Mississippi who, they knew, would soon move into the region. All this and more they put into their reports to the President and the secretary of war. They knew that if their precious shipment reached Washington it would in one swoop reveal more to the lay and scientific world about the sixteen hundred miles of the Missouri Valley they had traveled than had been disseminated since the first white men had coursed through the region nearly a century earlier.

The shipment more than satisfied Jefferson's stringent instructions. Still, it must to a degree have embarrassed Lewis. He contributed his record of astronomical observations, an essay on Indian tribes, and "A Summary View of the Rivers and Creeks" entering the Missouri, which was an elaboration of Clark's tabular "Sum-

Indians Hunting the Bison, aquatint of watercolor by Karl Bodmer
RARE BOOK DIVISION, THE NEW YORK PUBLIC LIBRARY,
ASTOR, LENOX AND TILDEN FOUNDATIONS

mary Statement of Rivers and Creeks." The map of the Missouri
thus far covered, a projection of the route westward to the Rocky
Mountains, the daily meteorological record, the elaborate chart of
Indian tribes inhabiting the Missouri Valley, the daily journal of
happenings along the way—all came from Clark's pen. Even the
"invoice of articles forwarded from Fort Mandan to the President
of the United States" was in his hand. That part of the cargo,
whose packing Clark probably supervised, consisted of four boxes,
a large trunk, and three cages. In the cages were a live prairie dog,
a sharp-tailed grouse, then unknown to science, and four magpies.
In the boxes were the horns of a bighorn sheep and of a wapiti,
the skins and sometimes skeletons of antelopes, jack rabbits,
badgers, a coyote, and a grizzly bear—all but the grizzly, new to
science. (Also included were the skins of twelve red foxes. The
captains were unaware that, although the red fox did not live east
of the Mississippi, scientists had already identified it.) Scattered

Bison-dance of the Mandan Indians,
aquatint of watercolor by Karl Bodmer
RARE BOOK DIVISION, THE NEW YORK PUBLIC LIBRARY,
ASTOR, LENOX AND TILDEN FOUNDATIONS

through the boxes were several parcels of Indian artifacts, most of them acquired from the Mandans—a bow with a quiver of arrows, an earthen pot, samples of native tobacco seed, an ear of corn, various articles of dress, and several buffalo robes, one of which depicted a battle "fought eight years since by the Sioux and Ricaras against the Mandans, Minitris, and Ahwahharways." One of the boxes held sixty-seven specimens of "earths, salts, and minerals" and sixty pressed specimens of plants. The most polished scientist of the day could not have improved on Lewis' exemplary handling of these specimens. Each carried a label "expressing the days on which obtained, places where found and also their virtues and properties when known. By means of the labels reference may be made to the chart sent to the secretary of war, on which encampment of each day has been carefully marked."

The chart sent to the secretary of war was Clark's map of the Missouri. It held no startling revelations but its detail and precision

made all previous ones instantly obsolete. (Jefferson, who seemed
determined to ignore Clark's presence on the expedition, called it
"Lewis' large map" and said it consisted of "twenty-nine half sheets
which contain very accurately his survey of the river and no more.")
If the "and no more" was accurate, then Clark sent along a second
map on which he identified each day's encampment and also a
general indication of the territory claimed by the tribes scattered
through the Missouri Valley. The first of Jefferson's numerous instructions regarding the Indians had said, "you will . . . endeavor
to make yourself acquainted . . . with . . . the extent and limits
of their possessions."

The Indian tribes—fifty-three all told; not just the few met
coming up river but all the captains heard about from voyageurs,
the Indians themselves, and the French and English traders met at
Fort Mandan—were analyzed on a large chart Clark constructed out
of six sheets of paper which, when pasted together, extended over
a yard in length and two feet in width. The analysis was organized
around nineteen questions. From queries raised in Jefferson's instructions—what was each tribe's "relation with other tribes . . .
their language . . . their ordinary occupations . . .?"—the chart
branched into such matters as each tribe's nickname among Canadian fur traders, the number of its lodges, warriors, and overall
population; "the kind of peltries and robes which they annually
supply or furnish . . . the estimated amount of merchandise in
dollars, at the Saint Louis prices . . . the names of the nations
with whom they are at war . . . the names of the nations with
whom they maintain a friendly alliance . . . the particular water
courses on which they reside or rove . . . the place at which it
would be mutually advantageous to form the principal establishment in order to supply the several nations with merchandise."
Material that did not fit under these rubrics was supplied in the
essay by Lewis, which went with the chart to the President. The
essay gave room for personal judgments. On the chart the Teton
Sioux appear to differ little from their neighbors, but in the accompanying comments by Lewis they blossom forth as "the vilest

miscreants of the savage race," a tribe governed by the thought that "The more illy they treat the traders, the greater quantity of merchandise they will bring them, and that they will thus obtain the articles they wish on better terms."

(Clark seemed happiest when dealing with facts and figures that left no room for personal opinions.) To chart the twists and turns, the depths and widths of the Missouri, to list in neat array the number of warriors, lodges, horses, the enemies, and friends of an Indian tribe, satisfied his need for expression. Lewis, on the other hand, liked to speculate and preferred to inject something of himself in his reports. Clark's list of the rivers and creeks that discharged into the Missouri noted the width of each, its latitude, its distance from Saint Louis. A column headed "remarks" gave room to expand on his statistics; instead he allowed himself only a descriptive word or two—"small," "abandoned," "bold stream." Lewis took this succinct report and elaborated it into a graceful essay wherein, among other things, he speculated about the country stretching away from the Missouri and through which these streams flowed.

Lewis and Clark worked together through the winter trying to sift fact from legend about the route into the unknown. Clark embodied the findings in a series of tentative maps which he revised after each talk with an Indian chief or a Canadian trader until in the early spring he had one he thought accurate enough to send to the President. Lewis put his thoughts into an essay. The first major landmark would be the Yellowstone River. Clark, on a chart of the Missouri's "subsidiary streams higher up," noted that the Yellowstone at its mouth was four hundred yards wide, that it joined the Missouri from the southwest, that it lay 220 miles west of Fort Mandan, 1,850 upriver from Saint Louis. None of these figures showed up in Lewis' comments about the river. "If Indian information can be relied on," he wrote, "this river waters one of the fairest portions of Louisiana, a country not yet hunted, and abounding in animals of the fur kind." As a Jefferson-trained geopolitician, he sensed that the spot where the Yellowstone joined the Missouri was of decisive importance. To block expansion of the aggressive Northwest Company of Canada, the United States must build a trading post there. "If this powerful and ambitious company are suffered uninterruptedly to prosecute their trade with the nations inhabiting the upper portion of the Missouri, and thus acquire an influence with those people, it is not difficult to conceive the obstructions which they might hereafter through the medium of that influence, oppose to the will of our government or the navigation of the Missouri."

After passing the "river that scolds all others," 150 miles west of the Yellowstone, exactly 2,000 miles from Saint Louis as Clark figured it, and after the Musselshell River, another 120 miles farther along, the party would come to a second key landmark 570 miles west of Fort Mandan—the great falls.

This is described by the Indians as a most tremendous cataract. They state that the noise it makes can be heard at a great distance, that the whole body of the river tumbles over a precipice of solid and even rock many feet high; that such is the velocity of the water before it arrives at the precipice that it projects itself many feet beyond the base of the rock between which, and itself, it leaves a vacancy sufficiently wide for several persons to pass abreast underneath the torrent from bank to bank without wetting their feet. They also state that there is a fine open plain on the north side of the falls through which canoes and baggage may be readily transported. This portage, they assert, is no greater than half a mile, and that the river then assumes its usual appearance, even being perfectly navigable.

Seventy-five miles beyond the Great Falls the party would come to the Rocky Mountains. The Indians' description made it clear they were higher than eastern mountains but, if Lewis and Clark understood them correctly, not much more intimidating. They stretched from north to south in four great chains separated by wide, fertile valleys. The Missouri meandered through the first three chains much as the Shenandoah and Potomac did through

A Mandan Village, aquatint of watercolor by Karl Bodmer

the Appalachians. Just beyond the third chain the river, still navigable, split into three forks. The party should take the northern fork, which would carry them to the foot of the fourth chain, "which divides the waters of the Atlantic from those of the Pacific Ocean." A half-day, fifteen-mile portage would carry the expedition "to a large river which washes its western base." On that river they would meet Indians who lived "principally on a large fish . . . the salmon, with which we are informed the Columbia River abounds."

The captains could count on a short half-day portage despite the mountain of goods and provisions the party would carry because they knew they would have horses to speed them along. Almost immediately upon landing among the Mandans and Minitaris they had learned that the Snake Indians (as Lewis and Clark called them; today they are called Shoshoni), who lived on the eastern slopes of the Rocky Mountains, had large herds of excellent horses.

Each spring when the Snakes came down from their mountain retreats to hunt buffalo on the plains, the Minitris raided them. When they returned to their lodges on the Missouri they occasionally brought back a captive or two along with the plundered horses. Five years earlier they had returned with a slip of a girl who now, as a young lady of sixteen or seventeen, carried the child of her husband Touissant Charbonneau, a French *voyageur*. When Charbonneau offered to join the expedition as an interpreter the captains, despite his drawbacks—he was forty-four years old, barely spoke English, and was filled with self-importance—took him on, with the understanding that his young wife, Sacagawea, would come along "to interpret the Snake language." Apparently it did not bother them she was then six months pregnant. She gave birth "to a fine boy" on February 11. Her "labor was tedious and the pain violent," which belied the myth that Indian women gave birth easily. During her labor a French *voyageur* told Lewis that he had "frequently administered a small portion of the rattle of the rattlesnake, which he assured me had never failed to produce the desired effect—that of hastening the birth of the child. Having the rattle of a snake by me I gave it to him and he administered two rings of it to the woman broken in small pieces with the fingers and added to a small quantity of water." She had "not taken it more than ten minutes before she brought forth." Lewis was impressed, "but I must confess that I want faith as to its efficacy."

The captains seemed unconcerned about carrying a nursing infant into the unknown. Charbonneau, though, gave them pause. A month after his son's birth he announced he would serve only as interpreter on the trip. "He will not agree to work, let our situation be what it may, nor stand a guard, and if miffed with any man he wishes to return when he pleases; also have the disposal of as much provisions as he chooses to carry." The captains sent him packing. Charbonneau brooded a few days, then told Lewis and Clark that he was "sorry for the foolish part he had acted and if we pleased he would accompany us agreeably to the terms we had proposed and do everything we wished him to do, etc., etc."

Charbonneau's retreat came as the crew made final preparations for departure into the unknown. Six dugouts had been hacked out of a stand of cottonwoods. Cracks in the windshaken trunks had been caulked and covered with strips of tin. The two pirogues had been refurbished after a winter of being battered by river ice. "All the party in high spirits," Clark remarked on March 31. "They pass but few nights without amusing themselves dancing, possessing perfect harmony and good understanding towards each other. Generally healthy except for venereals complaints which is very common amongst the natives and the men catch it from them."

On Sunday, 7 April 1805, at four o'clock in the afternoon the barge, manned by six soldiers under the command of Corporal Warfington, set out downstream with its precious cargo for President Jefferson and the secretary of war. "At the same time," Clark noted matter-of-factly in his journal, "we set out on our voyage up the river," and after listing members of the expedition ended his entry for the day. Lewis could not let so dramatic a moment pass unnoticed.

Our vessels consisted of six small canoes and two large pirogues. This little fleet, altho' not quite so respectable as those of Columbus or Captain Cook, were still viewed by us with as much pleasure as those deservedly famed adventurers ever beheld theirs; and I dare say with quite as much anxiety for their safety and preservation. We are now about to penetrate a country at least two thousand miles in width, on which the foot of civilized man had never trodden; the good or evil it had in store for us was for experiment yet to determine, and these little vessels contained every article by which we were to expect to subsist or defend ourselves. However, as the state of mind in which we are generally gives the coloring to events, when the imagination is suffered to wander into futurity, the picture which now presented itself to me was a most pleasing one. Entertaining as I do the most confident hope of succeeding in a voyage which had formed a darling project of mine for the last ten years, I could but esteem this moment of my departure as among the most happy of my life. The party are in excellent health and spirits, zealously attached to the enterprise, and anxious to proceed; not a whisper of murmur or discontent to be heard among them, but all act in unison, and with the most perfect harmony. I took an early supper this evening and went to bed.

Part Three

Into the Unknown

Chapter 11

"A Verry Large
and Turrible Animal"

The land remained much as it had been—the treeless plains still stretched away to the horizons, the twisting river was still lined with cottonwoods that shrouded an undergrowth of wild roses and a variety of berry bushes. Only now the great flocks of geese and ducks that flew overhead were northbound; the wild cherries and plum bushes were in bloom; the cottonwoods had begun to leaf, and the prairies tc shade from their winter brown to a light green. Spring, fickle as always, one morning brought delightful weather, the next a cold snap that left the men's oars rimmed with ice. But each new day saw winter pushed farther behind.

The crew had been freed from the oppressive bulk of the barge, but they still had a hard time pushing up the river. Crumbling banks continued to endanger the lives of everyone, and twice boats were almost buried beneath them. The wind blew steadily and "with astonishing violence." It churned up waves that nearly swamped the overloaded dugouts and several times forced the party to lay ashore until it had abated. The sandy topsoil of the plains stirred up by the wind created a curtain of pricking particles for the men to row through. "So penetrating is this sand that we cannot keep any article free from it. In short, we are compelled to eat, drink, and breathe it freely."

Occasionally the wind worked in the party's favor and those on the two pirogues could raise the sails—a square sail amidship, a spritsail on the bow—and these carried them along "at a pretty good gait." The fifth day out from Fort Mandan Charbonneau was steering the white pirogue under sail when a burst of wind swung the boat about. Charbonneau panicked and nearly overturned the craft. "This accident was very nearly costing us dearly. Believing this vessel to be the most steady and safe, we had embarked on board it our instruments, papers, medicine, and the most valuable part of the merchandise which we had still in reserve as presents for the Indians. We had also embarked on board ourselves, with three men who could not swim, and the squaw with the young child, all of whom, had the pirogue overset, would most probably have perished, as the waves were high and the pirogue upwards of two hundred yards from the nearest shore."

That same day the party saw tracks "of enormous size" of an animal they had long been waiting to meet—the great white or brown or yellow bear—the color of its pelt varied and so they were uncertain what to call it. The Mandan Indians had given them "a very formidable account of the strength and ferocity of this animal." Slaying one equated killing an enemy in battle, so far as the Indians were concerned. They only ventured out against the beast "in parties of six, eight, or ten persons, and are even then frequently defeated with the loss of one or more of their party." These tales did not especially impress Lewis or Clark. The Indians had only bows and arrows "and the indifferent guns with which the traders furnish them," and with those weapons they "shoot with such uncertainty and at so short a distance that they frequently miss

Hunting of the Grizzly Bear, aquatint of watercolor by Karl Bodmer
RARE BOOK DIVISION, THE NEW YORK PUBLIC LIBRARY,
ASTOR, LENOX AND TILDEN FOUNDATIONS

their aim and fall a sacrifice to the bear." The American rifle in the hands of American hunters obviously would dispatch the animal with ease. Still, "the men as well as ourselves are anxious to meet with some of these bear."

The party continued to see the immense tracks almost daily, usually around the carcasses of buffalo that had died during the winter trying to cross the river. Once or twice hunters spotted the bears, but when the men approached, the huge beasts ran—contrary to the Indians' assurance that they preferred to attack than to flee. The party concluded the bears were "extremely wary and shy" and that "the Indian account of them does not correspond with our experience so far."

Everything, not just the white bear's tracks, seemed outsized in this land of the big sky. The beaver, numerous now, were fatter, with thicker fur than any the party had ever seen. The size of the grazing herds of buffalo, sometimes as large as ten thousand animals, dwarfed those seen last year downstream. The tame-like nature of these animals contrasted with the supposed ferocity of the white bear. The beaver swam unconcernedly past the boats and peeped from their houses on side streams watching the curious caravan pass. "The buffalo, elk, and antelope are so gentle that we pass near them while feeding, without appearing to excite any alarm among them; and when we attract their attention, they frequently approach us more nearly to discover what we are, and in some instances pursue us a considerable distance apparently with that view." Up to now the herds had only wolves to fear. One day Clark saw a pack of wolves cut down a stray calf while its mother wedged into the tightening herd. "The cows only defend their young so long as they are able to keep up with the herd and seldom return any distance in search of them."

The captains had planned on making twenty to twenty-five miles a day up the river, but the relentless headwinds kept the daily average closer to fifteen miles. On April 26, the party came to the Yellowstone River, two hundred eighty miles west of Fort Mandan and within thirty miles of where the Indians had said it would flow into the Missouri. If the Indian reports continued to be this accurate, then the Rocky Mountains, which they said would require only a half day's portage, would present no problem. Everyone was "much pleased" to reach the Yellowstone, a spot "long wished for, and in order to add in some measure to the general pleasure which seemed to pervade our little community, we ordered a dram to be issued to each person; this soon produced the fiddle and they spent the evening with much hilarity, singing and dancing, and seemed as perfectly to forget their past toils as they appeared regardless of those to come."

Past the Yellowstone the low banks of the Missouri rose into bluffs upon which grew clumps of dwarf cedar and great quantities of sagebrush. High on one of the bluffs early one morning Clark, accompanied by two hunters, spotted a bighorn sheep with a faun. Tales heard back in Saint Louis of the animal's remarkable agility now became fact. As Clark and his men approached, "the noise we made alarmed them and they came down on the side of the bluff, which had but little slope, being nearly perpendicular." The hunters had two shots at the doe and missed both times. "Those animals ran and skipped about with great ease on this declivity and appeared to prefer it to the level bottom or plain."

Clark's disappointment was eased back in camp, where he found the party examining the carcass of a white bear. Lewis and a hunter had come upon a pair of them that afternoon and wounded both. One escaped; the other chased Lewis "seventy or eighty yards, but fortunately had been so badly wounded that he was unable to pursue me so closely as to prevent my charging my gun; we again repeated our fire and killed him." The color of the bear's fur was puzzling. It was not white but a shade somewhere between brown and yellow. The grizzly bear Mackenzie had talked about in his book had had white fur; this must be a different species. Certainly it was like no bear the men had seen before. The one Lewis had shot was much larger than any eastern black bear he had seen—though obviously a youngster it weighed at least three hundred pounds—its talons were larger and longer, its fur finer and thicker. Also, Lewis admitted, it was a "much more furious and formidable animal, and will frequently pursue the hunter when wounded," as the Indians had said. "It is astonishing to see the wounds they will bear before they can be put to death." "But," Lewis added, "in the hands of skillful riflemen they are by no means so formidable or dangerous as they have been presented."

Six days later, on May 5, he revised that lighthearted judgment when Clark and Drouillard came upon a huge bear—"a verry large and turrible looking animal." They put ten shots into him, five of them through the lungs, but he still had enough life to swim to a sandbar in mid-river and there, "making the most tremendous roaring," writhed on the ground for over twenty minutes before dying. Clark thought he weighed about five hundred pounds but everyone else mentally brought him in at six hundred pounds or more. Stretched out he measured eight feet seven and a half

Funeral Scaffold of a Sioux Chief,
aquatint of watercolor by Karl Bodmer

inches from nose to toe, five feet ten and a half inches around the chest, three feet eleven inches around the neck. "I find," said Lewis, "that the curiosity of our party is pretty well satisfied with respect to this animal. The formidable appearance . . . added to the difficulty with which they die when even shot through the vital parts, has staggered the resolution of several of them. Others, however, seem keen for action with the bear. I expect these gentlemen will give us some amusement shortly as they [the bears] soon begin to copulate."

Six days later Bratton raced into camp and after regaining his breath said a bear he had shot through the lungs had chased him for a half mile. "These bear being so hard to die rather intimidates us all," Lewis said. "I must confess that I do not like the gentlemen and had rather fight two Indians than one bear." Indeed, he went on, "I have therefore come to a resolution to act on the defensive only should I meet these gentlemen in the open country." By now the men knew they had no chance to kill a grizzly with a single shot except through the brains, "and this becomes difficult in consequence of two large muscles which cover the sides of the forehead and the sharp projection of the center of the frontal bone, which is also of a pretty good thickness."

On May 14, three days after Bratton's escape, came another adventure with the white-brown-yellow bear that Lewis thought called for a full report.

In the evening [he wrote], the men in two of the rear canoes discovered a large brown bear lying in the open grounds about three hundred paces from the river, and six of them went out to attack him, all good hunters. They took the advantage of a small eminence which concealed them and got within forty paces of him unperceived. Two of them reserved their fires, as he had been previously concerted; the four others fired nearly at the same time and put each his bullet through him. Two of the balls passed through the bulk of both lobes of his lungs. In an instant this monster ran at them with open mouth. The two who had reserved their fires discharged their pieces at him as he came towards them. Both of them struck him, one only slightly and the other fortunately broke his shoulder. This, however, only retarded his motion for a moment only. The men, unable to load their guns, took flight. The bear pursued and had very nearly overtaken them before they reached the river. Two of the party betook themselves to a canoe and the others separated and concealed themselves among the willows, reloaded their pieces. Each discharged his piece at him as they had an opportunity. They struck him several times again but the guns served only to direct the bear to them. In this manner he pursued two of them separately so close that they were obliged to throw aside their guns and pouches and throw themselves into the river, although the bank was nearly twenty feet perpendicular. So enraged was this animal that he plunged into

An American having struck a Bear but not killed him, escapes into a Tree.

Quaint rendering of a man treed by a bear,
from the journals of Patrick Gass

the river only a few feet behind the second man he had compelled to take refuge in the water, when one of those who still remained on shore shot him through the head and finally killed him. They then took him on shore and butchered him, when they found eight balls had passed through him in different directions. The bear being old, the flesh was indifferent. They therefore only took the skin and fleece. The latter made us several gallons of oil.

Soon every hunter had a tale to tell about the bear. Joseph Field stumbled upon one so near that a swipe of a paw struck Field's foot. Another, hidden in brush, rushed McNeal. The bear raised up on his back feet; McNeal clubbed him over the head with the butt of his musket. "The bear, stunned with the stroke, fell to the ground and began to scratch his head with his feet."

McNeal ran for sanctuary in a tree. "The bear waited at the foot of the tree until late in the evening before he left" and let McNeal escape back to camp.

Everyone in the party continued to call the animal the white or brown or yellow bear, depending on the specimen most recently shot, but months later when a long, wet winter by the Pacific Ocean gave the captains time to think about what they had seen the past year, they decided that the ferocious bear they had met east of the Rockies—it vanished on the western slopes of the mountains—was of the same family as the formidable grizzly bear Mackenzie had encountered in Canada "with a merely accidental difference in point of color."

Chapter 12

Gourmands

When Lewis and Clark erred, they did so on a grand scale. They learned nothing from the near-disaster in mid-April when the white pirogue, with Charbonneau at the helm, had nearly sunk with the bulk of their valuables aboard. A month later found Charbonneau, "perhaps the most timid waterman in the world," again at the helm of the white pirogue, which was again loaded with "our papers, instruments, books, medicine, a great part of our merchandise, and in short almost every article indispensably necessary to further the views or insure the success of the enterprise." And again the boat was under sail when again a sudden squall swept up the river. Again, Charbonneau panicked and let the pirogue luff up into the wind. "The wind was so violent that it drew the brace of the square sail out of the hand of the man who was attending it and instantly upset the pirogue and would have turned her completely had it not have been [for] the resistance made by the awning against the water." It took the crew nearly a minute to pull in the sail and right the boat, by then filled to the gunwales with water. "Charbonneau, still crying to his God for mercy, had not yet recollected the rudder, nor could the repeated orders of the bowman, Cruzatte, bring him to his recollection until he threatened to shoot him instantly if he did not take hold of the rudder and do his duty. The waves by this time were running very high, but the fortitude, resolution, and good conduct of Cruzatte.saved her. He ordered two men to throw out the water with some kettles that fortunately were convenient while himself and two others rowed her ashore, where she arrived scarcely above the water." The captains ended the day giving each man a dram of ardent spirits. No hint of a reprimand for Charbonneau appeared in the journals, but clearly his sailing days were over.

Lewis regarded Charbonneau in his final report to the War Department as "a man of no peculiar merit," yet he, Clark, and the crew tolerated him out to the Pacific and back—perhaps for the touch of comic relief he gave to trying days. Watching the voluble Frenchman "crying to his God for mercy" in the midst of catastrophe could only have brought smiles to the onlookers. He gave a Gallic flair to whatever he did, but his grandest performances came when, as stand-in cook, he served up a specialty, *boudin blanc*. While preparing his *pièce de résistance* he transformed before the crew's very eyes the backdrop of a rushing river and treeless plain into a well-equipped Parisian kitchen. "The first morsel that the cook makes love to" was some six feet of the lower intestine of a buffalo. "This he holds fast at one end with the right hand, while with the forefinger and thumb of the left he gently compresses it and discharges what he says is *not good to eat*." The gut emptied, he returns to the buffalo. "The muscle lying underneath the shoulder blade next to the back and fillets are next sought. These are kneaded up very fine with a good portion of kidney suet. To this composition is then added a just proportion of pepper and salt and a small quantity of flour." Charbonneau now ties one end of the intestine fast, turns it inside out and then begins "with repeated evolutions of the hands and arm and a brisk motion of the finger and thumb to put in what he says is *bon pour manger*." The stuffed intestine is tied off at the other end and the plump coil is "then baptised with the Missouri with two dips and a flirt and bobbed into the kettle, from whence after it is well boiled it is taken and fried with bear's oil until it becomes brown, when it is ready to assuage the pang of a keen appetite or such as travelers in the wilderness are seldom at a loss for."

The crew's diet ran mostly to meat—great quantities of it each day. When game was scarce, they managed to make seven lean elk last three days, but in flush times when the animals were fat, it took at least a buffalo a day to feed the group, or four deer, or an elk and a deer—or, figured another way, eight to ten pounds of meat a day for each man, thus a minimum of about two hundred and fifty pounds of meat daily. The consumption sometimes amazed even Clark. Once, on a side-excursion with only ten men, one of the hunters brought in an elk for supper. "It may appear somewhat incredible," Clark reported next morning, "but so it is that the elk which was killed last evening was eaten except about eight pounds, which I directed to be taken along with the skin."

In the early spring when the animals were thin and stringy and "not very pleasant food," the crew took only the best pieces—the tongue, marrowbones, a few fillets. Once calving season ended and fresh grass on the plains let the beasts fatten, the men dined well—on marbled buffalo beef, "deliciously flavored" antelope haunches, and, when they could bring one down, the "extremely delicate, tender and well-flavored" flesh of a bighorn sheep. The hunters shopped for dinner like housewives in a meat market. One afternoon Lewis "felt an inclination to eat some veal." He considered that of a young buffalo "equal to any veal I ever tasted," and after a short trip on shore he spotted "a very fine specimen, shot it, and had it for dinner. "We found the calf most excellent veal."

Except for a fat buffalo bull, the men preferred beaver over anything. Its flesh, said Lewis, "is esteemed a delicacy among us. I think the tail a most delicious morsel; when boiled it resembles in flavor the fresh tongues and sounds [swim-bladders] of the cod-fish and is sufficiently large to afford a plentiful meal for two men." Drouillard, as with everything involved with wilderness life, ex-celled at trapping beaver. He had a secret recipe that Lewis felt should be passed on to posterity. The male beaver had six stones, two of which—called bark stones or castors—would, "when prop-erly prepared," entice beavers from as far away as a mile, "their sense of smelling being very acute." Preparation of the stones was complicated. First,

the stone is taken at the base. This is gently pressed out of the bladderlike bag which contains it into a vial of four ounces with a wide mouth. If you have them, you will put from four to six stone in a vial of that capacity. To this you will add half a nutmeg, a dozen or fifteen grains of cloves, and thirty grains of cinnamon

Beaver Hut on the Missouri, aquatint of watercolor by Karl Bodmer

Trapping Beaver, watercolor by Jacob Alfred Miller
WALTERS ART GALLERY, BALTIMORE

finely pulverized. Stir them well together and then add as much
ardent spirits to the composition as will reduce it to the consistency
of mustard prepared for the table. When thus prepared it resembles mustard to all appearance. When you cannot procure a vial,
a bottle made of horn or a tight earthen vessel will answer. In all
cases it must be excluded from the air or it will soon lose its
virtue. It is fit for use immediately it is prepared but becomes
much stronger and better in about four or five days and will keep
for months provided it be perfectly secluded from the air. When
cloves are not to be had, use double the quantity of allspice, and
when no spice can be obtained use the bark of the root of sassa-
fras. When spirits cannot be had use oil stone of the beaver, adding merely a sufficient quantity to moisten the other materials or
reduce it to a stiff paste.

To this recipe Clark, in a footnote, added: "The bait is put on the
point of a stick and stuck in the ground so as the bait will be over
the trap which is under the water set for the beaver."

Sacagawea occasionally supplemented the meat diet with Indian recipes. The second day out from Fort Mandan she came
into camp with a skirt full of prairie turnips or "wild artichokes,"
or, as the engagés called them, pommes blanche. The men had
first tasted them among the Teton Sioux, but Sacagawea showed
how to find where prairie gophers had squirreled them away for
winter and how to cook them. Boiled, they resembled Jerusalem
artichokes. Lewis found "the white apple . . . to be a tasteless,
insipid food," although he knew "our epicures would admire this
root very much; it would serve them in their ragouts and gravies
instead of the truffles morella." The journals have little to say about
the matter, but once in a while the feeling comes through that
Sacagawea fussed around the campfire like a housewife in her
kitchen. "After eating the marrow out of two shank bones of an
elk," Clark remarks in one entry, "the squaw chopped the bones
fine, boiled them, and extracted a pint of grease, which is superior
to the tallow of the animal." More likely than not it was she, who
seemed to know everything that was edible in the wilderness, who
pointed out a wild onion "about the size of a small bullet," which,
when boiled, the men "found agreeable." Early in May she brought
to Clark a bush with a yellow flower which, she said, "bore a
delicious fruit and that great quantities grew on the Rocky Mountains."

From the end of May the party did not want for fresh fruit.
Below Fort Mandan the men had relished the "most delicious"
wild plums and the papaw or "custard apple, of which this country abounds and the men are very fond of." Now bushes ladened
with service berries and with currants—red, yellow, purple—lined
the banks. Lewis found "these fruits very pleasant, particularly the
yellow currant, which I think vastly preferable to those of our
gardens." Later, however, he came upon "a black currant which I
thought preferable in flavor to the yellow. This currant is really a
charming fruit and I am confident would be preferred at our markets to any currants now cultivated in the United States."

The party adjusted its menu and taste to whatever the changing countryside offered. Lewis waited until mid-July to sample "the small guts of the buffalo cooked over a blazing fire in the Indian style, without any preparation of washing or cleansing." He found them "very good." Later, close to starvation in the Rocky Mountains, the men reluctantly ate horsemeat. The "detestation and horror" first felt soon waned. "Thus," Lewis philosophized, "so soon is the mind which is occupied with any interesting object, reconciled to its situation."

New country invariably offered new delicacies for the palate. Across the Rockies Clark sampled his first salmon and judged it "the finest fish I ever tasted." Later, on the Pacific coast, he had to modify that judgment when he ate the eulachon, a species of smelt. "They are so fat that they required no additional sauce, and I think them superior to any fish I ever tasted, even more delicate and luscious than the white fish of the [Great] Lakes, which have heretofore formed my standard of excellence among the fishes. I have heard the fresh anchovy much extolled but I hope I shall be pardoned for believing this quite good."

One culinary delight—dogmeat—enjoyed by the others Clark could not stomach. "Our party," said Lewis, "from necessity having been obliged to subsist some length of time on dogs have now become extremely fond of their flesh. It is worthy of remark that while we lived principally on the flesh of this animal we were much more healthy, strong and more fleshy than we had been since we left the buffalo country. For my own part, I have become so perfectly reconciled to the dog that I think it an agreeable food and would prefer it vastly to lean venison or elk." Clark, after reading that entry of Lewis', said: "as for my own part, I have not become reconciled to the taste of this animal as yet."

Lewis liked almost anything put before him. Of the whale blubber found on the Pacific coast, he said: "It was white and not unlike the fat of pork, tho' the texture was more spongy and somewhat coarser. I had a part of it cooked and found it very palatable and tender. It resembled the beaver or the dog in flavor. It may appear somewhat extraordinary tho' it is a fact that the

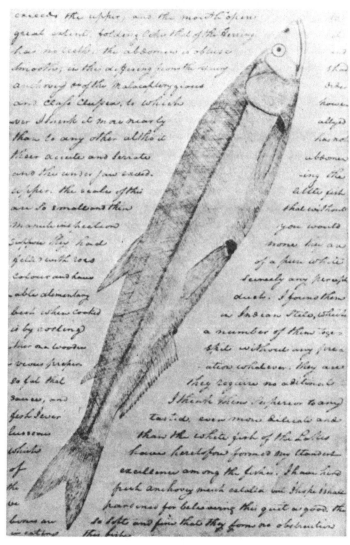

Clark's sketch of the Eulachon or Candlefish,
discovered February 24, 1806

flesh of the beaver and the dog possess a very great affinity in point of flavor." Clark copied the remark into his journal without comment. His taste buds were a puzzle. The same day a detachment assigned to distill salt from the ocean returned with several quarts of the precious item. "This was a great treat to myself and most of the party, having not had any since the 20th last," said Lewis. "I say most of the party, for my friend Capt. Clark declares it to be a mere matter of indifference with him whether he uses it or not. For myself I must confess I felt a considerable inconvenience from the want of it. The want of bread I consider as trivial provided I get fat meat, for as to the species of meat I am not particular—the flesh of the dog, the horse, and the wolf having from habit become equally familiar with any other. And I have learned to think that if the cord be sufficiently strong which binds the soul and body together it does not so much matter about the materials which compose it." Clark did not argue the point in his own journal.

Animals and plants flourished in the burgeoning spring as the Voyage of Discovery pushed and pulled its boats upriver toward the Rocky Mountains, past the River that Scolds All Others, which the captains renamed Milk River; past the Musselshell River, which lay about where the Indians said it would be—approximately five hundred miles west of Fort Mandan; past another "bold stream" which Clark, who rarely insisted on anything, insisted on naming the Judith, after a thirteen-year-old girl whom he planned to marry, and did three years later. By now the character of the Missouri had changed—for the worse, if that were possible. Its banks had risen into cliffs and the cliffs had spewed boulders into the stream that made progress slow, treacherous, and very painful. And as banks became cliffs, cottonwoods, as certain to be there as tomorrow, began to thin out and—incredible as it seemed—sometimes to disappear entirely. By the last week in May Lewis and Clark knew things looked "excessively bad."

Chapter 13

"Proceeded as Usual by the Cord"

26 May 1805

Set out at an early hour and proceeded principally by the tow-line, using the oars merely to pass the river in order to take advantage of the shores. Scarcely any bottoms to the river. The hills high and jutting in on both sides to the river in many places. . . .

Capt. Clark walked on shore this morning. . . . In the after part of the day I also walked out and ascended the river hills, which I found sufficiently fatiguing. On arriving to the summit of one of the highest points in the neighborhood I thought myself well repaid for my labor, as from this point I beheld the Rocky Mountains for the first time.* . . . While I viewed these mountains I felt a secret pleasure in finding myself so near the head

* He was wrong. Lewis saw the Highwood Mountains, east of Great Falls, Montana, according to John Logan Allen.

of the heretofore conceived boundless Missouri. But when I re-flected on the difficulties which this snowy barrier would most probably throw in my way to the Pacific, and the sufferings and hardships of myself and party in them, it in some measure counter-balanced the joy I had felt in the first moments in which I gazed on them. But as I have always held it a crime to anticipate evils, I will believe it a good comfortable road until I am compelled to believe differently. . . .

May 27

The wind blew so hard this morning that we did not [set] out until 10 A.M. We employed the cord most of the day. The river becomes more rapid and is intercepted by shoals and a greater number of rocky points at the mouths of the little gullies than we experienced yesterday. The bluffs are very high, steep, rugged, containing considerable quantities of stone and border the river closely on both sides. Once perhaps in the course of several miles there will be a few acres of tolerably level land in which two or three impoverished cottonwood trees will be seen. Great quantities of stone also lie in the river and garnish its borders, which appears to have tumbled from the bluffs where the rains had washed away the sand and clay in which they were embedded. . . .

This evening we encamped, for the benefit of wood, near two dead-topped cottonwood trees on the larboard side. The dead limbs which had fallen from these trees furnished us with a scanty sup-ply only, and more was not to be obtained in the neighborhood.

May 28

This morning we set forward at an early hour. The weather dark and cloudy, the air smoky, had a few drops of rain. We em-ployed the cord generally, to which we also gave the assistance of the pole at the riffles and rocky points. These are as numerous and many of them much worse than those we passed yesterday. Around those points the water drives with great force and we are obliged in many instances to steer our vessel through the apertures formed by the points of large sharp rocks which reach a few inches above the surface of the water. Here, should our cord give way, the bow is instantly driven outwards by the stream and the vessel thrown with her side on the rocks where she must inevitably overset or perhaps be dashed to pieces. Our ropes are but slender, all of them except one being made of elks' skin and much worn, frequently wet, and exposed to the heat of the weather are weak and rotten. They have given way several times in the course of the day but happily at such places that the vessel had room to wheel free of the rocks and therefore escaped injury. With every precaution we can take it is with much labor and infinite risk that we are enabled to get around these points. . . .

May 29

Last night we were all alarmed by a large buffalo bull, which swam over from the opposite shore and coming alongside of the white pirogue climbed over it to land. He, then alarmed, ran up the bank in full speed directly towards the fires, and was within eighteen inches of the heads of some of the men who lay sleeping before the sentinel could alarm him or make him change his course. Still more alarmed, he now took his direction immediately towards our lodge, passing between four fires and within a few inches of the heads of one range of the men as they yet lay sleeping. When he came near the tent, my dog saved us by causing him to change his course a second time, which he did by turning a little to the right, and was quickly out of sight, leaving us by this time all in an uproar with our guns in our hands, inquiring of each other the cause of the alarm, which after a few moments was explained by the sentinel. We were happy to find no one hurt. The next morning we found that the buffalo in passing the pirogue had trodden on a rifle which belonged to Capt. Clark's black man, who had negligently left her in the pirogue. The rifle was much bent. He had also broken the spindle, pivot, and shattered the stock of one of the blunderbusses on board. With this damage I felt well content, happy indeed that we had sustained no further injury. It appears that the white pirogue, which contains our valuable stores, is attended by some evil genie.

This morning we set out at an early hour and proceeded as usual by the cord. . . . At the distance of six and a half miles from our encampment of last night we passed a very bad rapid to which we gave the name of Ash Rapid from a few trees of that wood growing near them; this is the first ash I have seen for a great distance. At this place the hills again approach the river closely on both sides, and the same scene which we had on the 27th and 28th in the morning again presents itself, and the rocky points and riffles rather more numerous and worse. There was but little timber; salts, coal, etc., still appear.

Today we passed on the starboard side of the remains of . . . many mangled carcasses of buffalo which had been driven over a precipice of 120 feet by the Indians and perished. The water appeared to have washed away a part of this immense pile of slaughter and still there remained the fragments of at least a hundred carcasses. They created a most horrid stench. In this manner the Indians of the Missouri destroy vast herds of buffalo at a stroke. For this purpose one of the most active and fleet young men is selected and disguised in a robe of buffalo skin, having also the skin of the buffalo's head with the ears and horns fastened on his head in form of a cap. Thus caparisoned, he places himself at a convenient distance between a herd of buffalo and a precipice proper for the purpose, which happens in many places on the river for miles together. The other Indians now surround the herd on the back and flanks and at a signal agreed on all show themselves at the same time, moving forward towards the buffalo. The disguised Indian or decoy has taken care to place himself sufficiently nigh the buffalo to be noticed by them when they take to flight and running before them they follow him in full speed to the precipice, the cattle behind driving those in front over and seeing them go do not look or hesitate about following until the whole are precipitated down the precipice, forming one common mass of dead and mangled carcasses. The decoy in the meantime has taken care to secure himself in some cranny or crevice of the cliff which he had pre-

Hunting Buffalo, watercolor by Jacob Alfred Miller
WALTERS ART GALLERY, BALTIMORE

viously prepared for that purpose. The part of the decoy, I am informed, is extremely dangerous. If they are not very fleet runners,
the buffalo tread them under foot and crush them to death and
sometimes drive them over the precipice also, where they perish in
common with the buffalo.

We saw a great many wolves in the neighborhood of these
mangled carcasses. They were fat and extremely gentle. Capt. C.,
who was on shore, killed one of them with his espontoon.

Just above this place we came to for dinner opposite the
entrance of a bold running river forty yards wide, which falls in
on the larboard side. This stream we called Slaughter River. Its
bottoms are narrow and contain scarcely any timber. Our situation
was a narrow bottom on the starboard possessing some cottonwood.
Soon after we landed it began to blow and rain, and as there was
no appearance of even wood enough to make our fires for some
distance above we determined to remain here until the next morning, and accordingly fixed our camp and gave each man a small

dram. Notwithstanding the allowance of spirits we issued did not exceed a half [gill] per man, several of them were considerably affected by it. Such is the effects of abstaining for some time from the use of spirituous liquors. They were all very merry. The hunters killed an elk this evening and Capt. C. killed two beaver.

May 30

The rain which commenced last evening continued with little intermission until eleven this morning when we set out. The high wind which accompanied the rain rendered it impracticable to proceed earlier. More rain has now fallen than we have experienced since the 15 of September last. Many circumstances indicate our near approach to a country whose climate differs considerably from that in which we have been for many months. The air of the open country is astonishingly dry as well as pure. I found by several experiments that a tablespoon full of water exposed to the air in a saucer would evaporate in thirty-six hours when the mercury did not stand higher than the temperate point at the greatest heat of the day. My inkstand frequently becoming dry put me on this experiment. I also observed the well-seasoned case of my sextant shrunk considerably and the joints opened.

The water of the river still continues to become clearer, and notwithstanding the rain which has fallen it is still much clearer than it was a few days past.

This day we proceeded with more labor and difficulty than we have yet experienced. In addition to the embarrassment of the rapid current, riffles, and rocky points which were as bad if not worse than yesterday, the banks and sides of the bluff were more steep than usual and were now rendered so slippery by the late rain that the men could scracely walk. The cord is our only dependence, for the current is too rapid to be resisted with the oar and the river too deep in most places for the pole. The earth and stone also falling from these immense high bluffs render it dangerous to pass under them. The wind was also hard and against us. Our cords broke several times today but happily without injury to our vessels. We had slight showers of rain through the course of the day. The air was cold and rendered more disagreeable by the rain. . . . Two buffalo killed this evening a little above our encampment.

May 31

This morning we proceeded at an early hour with the two pirogues, leaving the canoes and crews to bring on the meat of the two buffalo that were killed last evening and which had not been brought in as it was late and a little off the river. Soon after we got underway it began to rain and continued until meridian when it ceased but still remained cloudy through the balance of the day. The obstructions of rocky points and riffles still continue as yesterday. At those places the men are compelled to be in the water even to their armpits and the water is yet very cold and so frequent are those points that they are one-fourth of their time in the water. Added to this the banks and bluffs along which they are obliged to pass are so slippery and the mud so tenacious that they are unable to wear their moccasins and in that situation dragging the heavy burthen of a canoe and walking occasionally for several hundred yards over the sharp fragments of rocks which tumble from the cliffs and garnish the borders of the river. In short, their labor is incredibly painful and great, yet those faithful fellows bear it without a murmur. The towrope of the white pirogue, the only one indeed of hemp, and that on which we most depended, gave way today at a bad point. The pirogue swung and but slightly touched a rock, yet was very near oversetting. I fear her evil genie will play so many pranks with her that she will go to the bottom some of those days.

Capt. C. walked on shore this morning but found it so excessively bad that he shortly returned. At twelve o'clock we came to for refreshment and gave the men a dram, which they received with much cheerfulness and well deserved.

Chapter 14

An Interesting Question Answered

On 2 June 1805, the Voyage of Discovery had come by Captain Clark's reckoning 2,508¼ miles up the Missouri when the caravan arrived at a bewildering fork in the river—one branch flowing in from the southwest, the other from the northwest. This posed "an interesting question." Which branch was the Missouri River that the Indians back at Fort Mandan "had described to us as approaching very near to the Columbia River?" The answer to the question must be right. "To mistake the stream at this period of the season, two months of the traveling season having now elapsed, and to ascend such stream to the Rocky Mountains or perhaps much farther before we could inform ourselves whether it did approach the Columbia or not, and then be obliged to return and take the other stream would not only lose us the whole of this season but would probably so dishearten the party that it might defeat the expedition altogether."

The answer to the question at first glance looked obvious. The two streams differed totally in character. The southern one flowed in clear and rapid with a smooth "unriffled surface," while the northern branch's turbid waters roiled and boiled along exactly like the Missouri the party had known the past year. "What astonishes us a little is that the Indians who appeared to be so well acquainted with the geography of this country should not have mentioned this river on right hand if it be not the Missouri." The voyage must halt and unravel the puzzle. None of the men objected, for "many of them have their feet so mangled and bruised with the stones and rough ground over which they passed barefoot that they can scarcely walk or stand."

The next morning the captains sent a canoe up each fork to chart its bearings. Leaving Sergeant Ordway as usual in charge of the camp, Lewis and Clark strolled to the top of a nearby hill. The day was pleasant and fair. They walked through clumps of chokeberries and gooseberries, yellow and red currants, all beginning to ripen. The wild rose was in full bloom and made an immense garden of the river bottoms. From the hilltop they had a "most enchanting view" of the High Plains, which stretched away in every direction. Huge herds of grazing buffalo, "attended by their shepherds, the wolves," blotted the scene, along with smaller herds of elk; a scattering of male antelopes grazed away from the females, who grazed with their newborn calves. To the south they had their first stunning view of the Rocky Mountains. The range closest to them they could see was only "partially covered with snow," Lewis observed matter-of-factly in his journal. "Behind these mountains and at a great distance, a second and more lofty range of mountains appeared to stretch across the country in the same direction with the others, reaching from the west to the north of northwest, where their snowy tops lost themselves beneath the horizon. This last range was perfectly covered with snow." Neither man appeared to find the view inspiring, magnificent, or, to use Clark's favorite word, beautiful. Indeed, as long as the expedition has the Rocky Mountains in sight the word "beautiful" fails to appear in the journals.

That evening the captains talked over the puzzle of the forked river with the men. Most favored the muddy northern branch as the true Missouri. The captains wondered. They decided that at sunrise Clark with five men would go up the southern fork and Lewis with six up the northern. They would travel by land a day and a half, "or further if it should appear necessary to satisfy us more fully of the point in question." The evening ended with a dram of whisky passed out to everyone.

Clark carried out his assignment with dispatch. The first day a grizzly nearly killed Joseph Field; otherwise the excursion was uneventful. The character of the river remained as it was at the forks, a mountain stream that raced down a channel hemmed in by high bluffs. Its course, west by south, convinced Clark the second day out that it was the true Missouri. He carved his name on a tree and headed back to camp, forty miles downstream. His party reached the forks "much fatigued." Lewis's party also arrived "much fatigued" but two days later and to a camp "waiting our return with some anxiety for our safety."

Lewis' journey had begun pleasantly. A few miles from camp he discovered a new bird, which he described with such wonderful precision that ornithologists know he had discovered McCowan's longspur.

It is about the size of a large sparrow, of a dark brown color with some white feathers in the tail. This bird, or that which I take to be the male, rises into the air about sixty feet and supporting itself in the air with a brisk motion of the wings, sings very sweetly, has several shrill notes rather of the plaintive order which it frequently repeats and varies. After remaining stationary about a minute in his aerial station, he descends obliquely, occasionally pausing and accompanying his descension with a note something like twit twit twit. On the ground he is silent. Thirty or forty of these birds will be stationed in the air at a time in view. These larks, as I shall call

Clark's drawing of the sage grouse, discovered June 5, 1805

them, add much to the gaiety and cheerfulness of the scene. All those birds are now setting and laying their eggs in the plains. Their little nests are to be seen in great abundance as we pass.

A heavy rain the first night wet everyone to the skin. The temperature dropped sharply and all awoke shivering under a cloudy sky. Lewis unpacked his blanket coat "in order to keep myself comfortable, although walking." The wretched prickly pears pierced the men's moccasins and made walking painful. Drouillard shot six bucks. The party passed an enormous colony of "burrowing or barking squirrels," the largest yet seen. Lewis came upon another new bird, the sage grouse, which he called "the mountain cock or a large species of heath hen." The day, in short, passed routinely.

On the third day out, June 6, Lewis concluded, despite shaking heads from the men, that "this branch of the Missouri had its direction too much to the north for our route to the Pacific." He named it Maria's River, after a lovely cousin. (The name has since been standardized as Marias River.)

True, its muddy, boiling waters did not "comport with the pure celestial virtues" of that fair young lady, but it was a noble river, and it passed "through a rich, fertile, and one of the most beautifully picturesque countries that I ever beheld. . . . its borders garnished with one continued garden of roses, while its lofty and open forests are the habitation of myriads of the feathered tribes who salute the ear of the passing traveler with their wild and simple, yet sweet and cheerful melody." Also, it might one day be commercially and politically valuable if its northerly course led into the rich fur country now preempted by the British.

The Marias' Eden-like garden showed another side of its character on the trip back to camp. The party tried first rafting downstream but after several mishaps all agreed to abandon the river for land. They hiked through the undergrowth in a brisk, cold northeast storm. After a pause for the noon dinner, they made twenty-three soggy miles through the continuing rain. They had to camp in the open along the river. It rained all night. "Our camp possessing no allurements, we left our watery beds at an early hour and continued our route down the river."

The rain barely penetrated the hard soil of the river bluffs and made them slippery as ice to walk along. Lewis fell once and saved himself from a ninety-foot drop into the river by digging his espontoon into the ground. He had hardly regained safety when, from behind, Wiser cried, "God, God, captain, what shall I do?" Lewis swung round to see the man "lying prostrate on his belly, with his right hand, arm and leg over the precipice while he was holding on with his left arm and foot as well as he could, which appeared to be with much difficulty." Wiser's situation looked hopeless, but "I disguised my feelings and spoke very calmly to him and assured him that he was in no kind of danger, to take the knife out of his belt behind him with his right hand and dig a hole with it in the face of the bank to receive his right foot." Wiser did as told. Once on his knees, he took off his slippery moccasins, as Lewis directed, dug his knife into the soil and inched to safety.

The party left the glazed bluffs and spent the rest of the day "sometimes in the mud and water of the bottom lands, at others in the river to our breasts, and when the water became so deep that we could not wade we cut footsteps in the face of the steep bluffs with our knives and proceeded." They slogged eighteen miles to a happy ending. As darkness set in they came upon an abandoned Indian lodge "which afforded us a dry and comfortable shelter." They roasted the best pieces of four deer shot on the trek that day and ate heartily, "not having tasted a morsel before during the day." Dawn brought a clear sky and the revived Lewis noticed that the "birds appeared to be very gay and sung most enchantingly." The party reached camp at 5 P.M. and celebrated with drinks.

That evening Clark charted the courses of the two rivers as far as they had been explored. He and Lewis then studied Arrowsmith's map, which in its latest edition incorporated information brought back by Peter Fidler, an employee of Hudson's Bay Company who had traveled in the Rocky Mountain region a decade earlier. Fidler said he had been as far south as the forty-fifth parallel and seen no great streams pouring eastward from the mountains. But the Voyage of Discovery now camped at the forty-seventh parallel. If the observations of Fidler, a trained surveyor, were accurate that meant the Missouri must emerge from the mountains far to the south. Yet the excursion up the south fork had convinced Clark its course ran closer to west than south.

Facts gleaned from the Indians also contradicted Fidler. They had said the Missouri came from the mountains, that its waters would become transparent as the party approached a series of waterfalls, and that those falls lay a little south of sunset, which translated into latitude approximated where the expedition now camped. But some puzzling aspects muddied the Indians' information. As Clark had understood their estimates, they had said the Great Falls lay 610 miles west of Fort Mandan, yet the party had already traveled 800 miles. And if the south fork were the Missouri, why had they failed to mention the Marias?

The captains resolved before carrying these questions to bed that whichever fork they took neither could be navigated by the large red pirogue. The next morning, while they huddled over maps and notes, the pirogue's seven-man crew prepared to bury its contents in what the engagés called a "cache." Pierre Cruzatte, being "well acquainted with this business," oversaw the operation. His ingenious creation impressed all.

It is in a high plain about forty yards distant from a steep bluff of the south branch on its northern side; the situation a dry one, which is always necessary. A place being fixed on for a cache, a circle of about twenty inches in diameter is first described. The turf or sod of this circle is carefully removed, being taken out as entire as possible in order that it may be replaced in the same situation when the cache is filled and secured. This circular hole is then sunk perpendicularly to the depth of one foot; if the ground be not firm somewhat deeper. They then begin to work it out wider as they proceed downwards until they get it about six or seven feet deep, giving it nearly the shape of the kettle or lower part of a large still. Its bottom is also somewhat sunk in the center. The dimensions of the cache is in proportion to the quantity of articles intended to be deposited. As the earth is dug, it is handed up in a vessel and carefully laid on a skin or cloth and then carried to some place where it can be thrown in such manner as to conceal it, usually into some running stream where it is washed away and leaves no traces which might lead to the discovery of the cache.

Before the goods are deposited they must be well dried. A parcel of small dry sticks are then collected and with them a floor is made of three or four inches thick which is then covered with some dry hay or a rawhide well dried. On this the articles are deposited, taking care to keep them from touching the walls by putting other dry sticks between as you stow away the merchandise. When nearly full the goods are covered with a skin and earth thrown in and well rammed until with the addition of the turf first removed the whole is on a level with the surface of the ground. In this manner dried skins or merchandise will keep perfectly sound for several years.

The cache completed, the men gathered to hear the captains' answer to the interesting question posed by the forks. The leaders said they had decided to trust the red rather than the white man. Fidler must have erred in his observations. Indian accounts of the approach to the Rocky Mountains were too circumstantial to be dismissed. Moreover, the very consistency of character between the Marias and the Missouri the party had known thus far indicated it must emerge out of the plains, not the mountains. The south fork must be the Missouri. The crew to a man disagreed. Old Cruzatte, whose "integrity, knowledge, and skill as a waterman had acquired the confidence of every individual of the party," spoke for them: "the north fork was the true, genuine Missouri and could be no other." Even so, as a testament of their respect for the captains, the men said "very cheerfully that they were ready to follow us anywhere we thought proper to direct."

After Cruzatte spoke up, the captains conferred and decided that Lewis, traveling lightly with four men, would move ahead day after next by land in search of the Great Falls, while Clark, "the best waterman," brought the caravan up the river. They gave the decision to the crew, then judiciously passed out a dram of whisky. Cruzatte brought forth his fiddle, and the men "amused themselves dancing and singing songs in the most social manner," or, as one of them put it, "we had a frolic."

The next day was given over to travel preparations. The ingenious Shields unpacked his forge and conjured up a new main-spring for Lewis' air gun. The large red pirogue was stashed on an island in the river and covered with branches to protect it from the sun. Another cache was made. Into it went some provisions—a keg of flour, two kegs of parched meal, two kegs of pork, one keg of salt, a set of carpenter's tools, Shields' forge and blacksmith tools, and whatever superfulous items the men could be persuaded to part with—buffalo robes, beaver skins, the horns of a mountain sheep, and other souvenirs picked up along the way. All told they buried over a thousand pounds of baggage. Lewis passed part of the day hiking through the countryside and came upon another new bird, the white rumped shrike.

The advance party set out at 8 A.M. on June 11, walking toward a horizon rimmed with range upon range of snow-topped mountains—"an august spectacle still rendered more formidable by the recollection that we had to pass them." Shortly before noon two days later Lewis, moving ahead of the men, found his ears "saluted with the agreeable sound of a fall of water, and advancing a little farther I saw the spray arise above the plain like a column of smoke." Minutes later he heard a roar "too tremendous to be mistaken for any cause short of the Great Falls of the Missouri." He rushed down from the hill he had been traveling along to behold "a smooth, even sheet of water falling over a precipice of at least eighty feet." He rhapsodized over the "sublimely grand spectacle." Oh! if only he were a painter or a poet he could "give to the enlightened world some just idea of this truly magnificent and sublimely grand object which has from the commencement of time been concealed from the view of civilized man." Joseph Field, aware he would be among those who must lug the tons of baggage and heavy dugouts around the falls, reacted less eloquently. The next day back with the boats he said, when asked about the falls, "very bad."

Waterfalls

Chapter 15

The Great Falls

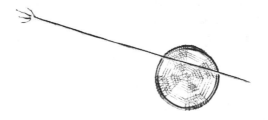

14 June 1805

This morning at sunrise I dispatched Joseph Field with a letter to Capt. Clark and ordered him to keep sufficiently near the river to observe its situation in order that he might be enabled to give Capt. Clark an idea of the point at which it would be best to halt to make our portage. I set one man about preparing a scaffold and collecting wood to dry the meat. Sent the others to bring in the balance of the buffalo meat, or at least the part which the wolves had left us, for those fellows are ever at hand and ready to partake with us the moment we kill a buffalo; and there is no means of putting the meat out of their reach in these plains. The two men shortly after returned with the meat and informed me that the wolves had devoured the great part of the meat.

About 10 o'clock this morning while the men were engaged with the meat I took my gun and espontoon and thought I would walk a few miles and see where the rapids terminated above and return to dinner. Accordingly, I set out and proceeded up the river about southwest. After passing one continued rapid and three small cascades of about four or five feet each at the distance of about five miles I arrived at a fall of about nineteen feet. The river here is about 400 yards wide. This pitch [the second falls], which I called "the crooked falls," occupies about three-fourths of the width of the river commencing on the south side, extends obliquely upwards about 150 yards, then forming an acute angle extends downwards nearly to the commencement of four small islands lying near the north shore. Among these islands and between them and the lower extremity of the perpendicular pitch, being a distance of 100 yards, the water glides down the side of a sloping rock with a velocity almost equal to that of its perpendicular descent. Just above this rapid the river makes a sudden bend to the right or northwardly.

I should have returned from hence, but hearing a tremendous roaring above me I continued my route across the point of a hill a few hundred yards farther and was again presented by one of the most beautiful objects in nature, a cascade of about fifty feet perpendicular [the third falls] stretching at right angles across the river from side to side to the distance of at least a quarter of a mile. Here the river pitches over a shelving rock, with an edge as regular and as straight as if formed by art, without a niche or break in it. The water descends in one even and uninterrupted sheet to the bottom where, dashing against the rocky bottom, it rises into foaming billows of great height and rapidly glides away, hissing, flashing, and sparkling as it departs. The spray rises from one extremity to the other to fifty feet. I now thought that if a skillful painter had been asked to make a beautiful cascade that he would most probably have presented the precise image of this one; nor could I for some time determine on which of those two great cataracts to bestow the palm, on this or that which I had discovered yesterday. At length I determined between these two great rivals for glory that this was pleasingly beautiful, while the other was sublimely grand.

I had scarcely unfixed my eyes from this pleasing object before I discovered another fall [number four] above at the distance of half a mile. Thus invited I did not once think of returning but hurried thither to amuse myself with this newly discovered object. I found this to be a cascade of about fourteen feet, possessing a perpendicular pitch of about six feet. This was tolerably regular, stretching across the river from bank to bank, where it was about a quarter of a mile wide. In any other neighborhood but this such a cascade would probably be extolled for its beauty and magnificence, but here I passed it by with but little attention; determining as I had proceeded so far to continue my route to the head of the rapids if it should even detain me all night.

At every rapid, cataract and cascade I discovered that the bluffs grew lower or that the bed of the river rose nearer to a level with the plains.

Still pursuing the river with its course about southwest, passing a continued scene of rapids and small cascades, at the distance of two and a half miles I arrived at another cataract [the fifth and last] of twenty-six feet. This is not immediately perpendicular; a rock about one-third of its descent seems to protrude to a small distance and receives the water in its passage downwards and gives a curve to the water, tho' it falls mostly with a regular and smooth sheet. The river is near six hundred yards wide at this place, a beautiful level plain on the south side only a few feet above the level of the pitch. On the north side, where I am, the country is more broken and immediately behind me near the river a high hill. Below this fall at a little distance a beautiful little island, well timbered, is situated about the middle of the river. In this island on a cottonwood tree an eagle has placed her nest. A more inaccessible spot I believe she could not have found; for neither man nor beast dare pass those gulfs which separate her little domain from the shores. The water is also broken in such manner as it descends over this pitch that the mist or spray rises to a considerable height. This fall is certainly much the greatest I ever beheld except those two which I have mentioned below. It is incomparably a greater cataract and a more noble, interesting object than the celebrated falls of Potomac or Schuylkill, etc.

Just above this is another cascade of about five feet, above which the water, as far as I could see, began to abate of its velocity, and I therefore determined to ascend the hill behind me which promised a fine prospect of the adjacent country. Nor was I disappointed on my arrival at its summit. From hence I overlooked a most beautiful and extensive plain, reaching from the river to the base of the snow-clad mountains to the south and southwest. I also observed the Missouri stretching its meandering course to the south through this plain to a great distance, filled to its even and grassy brim. Another large river flowed in on its western side about four miles above me and extended itself through a level and fertile valley of three miles in width a great distance to the northwest, rendered more conspicuous by the timber which garnished its borders. In these plains and more particularly in the valley just below me immense herds of buffalo are feeding. The Missouri just above this hill makes a bend to the south where it lies a smooth, even, and unruffled sheet of water of nearly a mile in width, bearing on its watery bosom vast flocks of geese which feed at pleasure in the delightful pasture on either border. The young geese are now completely feathered except the wings, which both in the young and old are yet deficient.

After feasting my eyes on this ravishing prospect and resting myself a few minutes, I determined to proceed as far as the river which I saw discharge itself on the west side of the Missouri, convinced that it was the river which the Indians call Medicine River and which they informed us fell into the Missouri just above the falls. I descended the hill and directed my course to the bend of the Missouri near which there was a herd of at least a thousand buffalo. Here I thought it would be well to kill a buffalo and leave him until my return from the river, and if I then found that I had not time to get back to camp this evening to remain all night here, there being a few sticks of driftwood lying along shore which would answer for my fire, and a few scattering cottonwood trees a few hundred yards below which would afford me at least the semblance of a shelter.

Under this impression I selected a fat buffalo and shot him very well through the lungs. While I was gazing attentively on the poor animal discharging blood in streams from his mouth and nostrils, expecting him to fall every instant, and having entirely forgotten to reload my rifle, a large white or rather brown bear had perceived and crept on me within twenty steps before I discovered him. In the first moment I drew up my gun to shoot, but at the same instant recollected that she was not loaded and that he was too near for me to hope to perform this operation before he reached me, as he was then briskly advancing on me. It was an open level plain, not a bush within miles nor a tree within less than three hundred yards of me. The river bank was sloping and not more than three feet above the level of the water. In short, there was no place by means of which I could conceal myself from this monster until I could charge my rifle.

In this situation I thought of retreating in a brisk walk as fast as he was advancing until I could reach a tree about three hundred yards below me. But I had no sooner turned myself about but he pitched at me, open mouthed and full speed. I ran about eighty yards and found he gained on me fast. I then ran into the water. The idea struck me to get into the water to such depth that I could stand and he would be obliged to swim and that I could in that situation defend myself with my espontoon. Accordingly, I ran hastily into the water about waist deep, and faced about and presented the point of my espontoon. At this instance he arrived at the edge of the water within about twenty feet of me. The moment I put myself in this attitude of defense he suddenly wheeled about, as if frightened, declined the combat on such unequal grounds and retreated with quite as great precipitation as he had just before pursued me. As soon as I saw him run off in that manner, I returned to the shore and charged my gun, which I had still retained in my hand throughout this curious adventure. I saw him run through the level open plain about three miles, till he disappeared

Bear vs Lewis

in the woods on Medicine River. During the whole of this distance he ran at full speed, sometimes appearing to look behind him as if he expected pursuit.

I now began to reflect on this novel occurrence and endeavored to account for this sudden retreat of the bear. I at first thought that perhaps he had not smelt me before he arrived at the water's edge so near me, but I then reflected that he had pursued me for about eighty or ninety yards before I took to the water and on examination saw the ground torn with his talons immediately on the impression of my steps; and the cause of his alarm still remains with me mysterious and unaccountable. So it was and I felt myself not a little gratified that he had declined combat.

My gun reloaded, I felt confidence once more in my strength; and determined not to be thwarted in my design of visiting Medicine River, but determined never again to suffer my piece to be longer empty than the time she necessarily required to charge her. I passed through the plain nearly in the direction which the bear had run to Medicine River, found it a handsome stream, about 200 yards wide with a gentle current, apparently deep, its waters clear, and [its] banks, which were formed principally of dark brown and blue clay, were about the height of those of the Missouri or from three to five feet. Yet they had not the appearance of ever being overflown, a circumstance which I did not expect so immediately in the neighborhood of the mountains, from whence I should have supposed that sudden and immense torrents would issue at certain seasons of the year; but the reverse is absolutely the case. I am therefore compelled to believe that the snowy mountains yield their waters slowly, being partially affected every day by the influence of the sun only, and never suddenly melted down by hasty showers of rain.

Having examined Medicine River, I now determined to return, having by my estimate about twelve miles to walk. I looked at my watch and found it was half after six P.M. In returning through the level bottom of Medicine River and about two hundred yards distant from the Missouri, my direction led me directly to an animal that I at first supposed was a wolf; but on nearer approach, or about sixty paces distant, I discovered that it was not. Its color was a brownish yellow. It was standing near its burrow and when I approached it thus nearly it crouched itself down like a cat, looking immediately at me as if it designed to spring on me. I took aim at it and fired. It instantly disappeared in its burrow. I loaded my gun and examined the place which was dusty and saw the track from which I am still further convinced that it was of the tiger kind [probably a wolverine, carcajou, or cougar]. Whether I struck it or not I could not determine, but I am almost confident that I did. My gun is true and I had a steady rest by means of my espontoon, which I have found very serviceable to me in this way in the open plains.

It now seemed to me that all the beasts of the neighborhood had made a league to destroy me, or that some fortune was disposed to amuse herself at my expense, for I had not proceeded more than three hundred yards from the burrow of this tiger cat before three bull buffalo, which were feeding with a large herd about a half mile from me on my left, separated from the herd and ran full speed towards me. I thought at least to give them some amusement and altered my direction to meet them. When they arrived within a hundred yards, they made a halt, took a good view of me and retreated with precipitation. I then continued my route homewards, passed the buffalo which I had killed but did not think it prudent to remain all night at this place, which really from the succession of curious adventures wore the impression on my mind of enchantment. At sometimes for a moment I thought it might be a dream, but the prickly pears which pierced my feet very severely once in a while, particularly after it grew dark, convinced me that I was really awake and that it was necessary to make the best of my way to camp.

It was sometime after dark before I returned to the party. I found them extremely uneasy for my safety. They had formed a thousand conjectures, all of which equally foreboding my death, which they had so far settled among them that they had already agreed on the route which each should take in the morning to search for me. I felt myself much fatigued but ate a hearty supper and took a good night's rest. The weather being warm, I had left my leather overshirt and had worn only a yellow flannel one.

Chapter 16

A Medical Case History

When Joseph Field returned to the boats with word that the Great Falls lay only twenty miles ahead, he found Captain Clark harassed by the racing river and by the very sick Sacagawea. Normally, Lewis served as the company's physician. Sacagawea had fallen ill before he departed, but she had become attached to Clark and chose him to cure her.

Clark bled Sacagawea on June 10. "Bleeding is proper at the beginning of all inflammatory fevers, as pleurisies, peripneumonies, etc.," according to a contemporary handbook. "It is likewise proper in all topical inflammations, as those of the intestines, womb, stomach, kidneys, . . . rheumatisms, the apoplexy, epilepsy, and the bloody flux." Or as the eminent Dr. Benjamin Rush put it, bleeding was obligatory "if the pulse be full and tense." A tense patient must be relaxed before any cure could be effected. The usual procedure was to cut open a vein—the medical chest Lewis had assembled in Philadelphia carried "three best lances" for the purpose but in an emergency a jackknife would and did do—on the inside of the elbow and let what the physicians deemed a sufficient amount of blood drip into a basin. The amount drained varied with the severity of the disease. The regimen "appeared to be of great service" to Sacagawea, Clark reported.

But on June 12 she continued "very *sick*, so much so that I move her into the back part of our covered part of the pirogue, which is cool, her own situation being a very hot one in the bottom of the pirogue exposed to the sun." She lay there listlessly nursing her infant son while the raging river pounded against the boat. The whole party worried about her. They were fond of her and the child, but they also knew that she was their "only dependence for a friendly negotiation with the Snake Indians, on whom we depend for horses to assist us in our portage from the Missouri to the Columbia River."

She continued ill on June 13. Clark gave her a dose of Glauber's salts, another standard remedy. Once relaxed the body must be cleansed of all "morbific matter." Still she refused to mend. She moaned all night and was "excessively bad" the next morning. Her pain, to Clark's embarrassment, centered in the uterus. Two of the men complained of toothaches and another had an inflamed tumor on his leg. Clark paid them no attention. The party had a packet of dentist tools to handle the toothaches if they continued, and tumors were routine irritants which time usually healed.

June 15 found the usually gay Sacawagea "low spirited." Her fever continued high and to relieve it Clark gave her a dose of bark—Jesuits bark or *cinchona*, a crude form of quinine. He also applied it externally to her uterus, or as he delicately put it, "her region." The rest of the day he had to give to the river, now almost a continuous rapid. "The fatigue which we have to encounter is incredible. The men in the water from morning until night hauling the cords and boats, walking on sharp rocks and round slippery stones, which alternately cut their feet and throw them down." They also had to contend with rattlesnakes. One man reaching for a branch found he had a rattler by the head and barely escaped being bitten. (Lewis at the falls awoke from a nap to find one coiled ten feet from his head. He killed it, then calmly counted the scuta—176 on the abdomen, 17 on the tail—and noted its coloring for his journal.) Despite all they endured, the men "go with cheerfulness."

Sacagawea worsened in the evening. She refused to take the medicine prescribed by Clark. Her husband, Charbonneau, begged Clark to turn the boats back to Fort Mandan. Clark ignored him, and the next morning pushed on to the foot of the Great Falls, where with relief he turned over his patient to Lewis. She was a pitiful sight, much wasted, lying in the stern of the pirogue with her child in her arms.

Lewis lacked formal medical training, but by the standards of the day was an accomplished physician. Dr. Rush had found little to add to the list of medical supplies and equipment he had drawn up for the expedition. Among the drugs Lewis had included fifteen pounds of the best powdered bark, ten pounds of Glauber's salts, four ounces of calomel, twelve ounces of opium, a quarter ounce of tarter emetic (this, to promote vomiting, a favorite of Rush; he raised the quantity to an ounce), a half pound of jalap (a powdered purgative made from a Mexican root), and two pounds of nitre or saltpeter, a diuretic that also induced sweat. Rush's main contribution to the medicine cabinet was fifty dozen pills of his own concoction, a powerful physic made up of ten grains of calomel and ten of jalap and commonly known as "Rush's thunderbolts."

Lewis' medical training had started as a boy. His mother was what people in the backcountry of the South called an "herb doctor." The eighteenth century believed that God had put nothing on earth in vain. For every disease that afflicted man a remedy flourished somewhere in the natural world. Herb doctors prescribed the foul-smelling, highly poisonous Jamestown weed smoked in a pipe to relieve asthma. Pokeberries served "as a plaster of great virtue for the cancer." The lance might relieve a bad sty on the eyelid, but first a rotten apple applied to the swelling ought to be

Western meadowlark, discovered June 22, 1805,
photograph of engraving by Audubon

tried. Lewis' encyclopedic knowledge of the flora of the South owed much to his years spent searching out medicinal plants for his mother. Like her, he had great faith in natural medicine. The second week on the trek up the Missouri he came upon what he called a "yellow root," and perhaps for her he put down the recipe of this sovereign remedy for "a violent inflammation of the eyes" that sometimes led to blindness.

Let the roots be gathered, washed, and carefully dried in the shade. Break them in pieces of half an inch in length, and put them in a bottle or vial, taking care to fill the vessel about two-thirds full of the dried root, then fill the vessel with cold water; rain water is preferable. Let it remain about six hours, shaking it occasionally, and it will be fit for use. The water must remain with the root and be applied to the eyes frequently by wetting a piece of fine linen and touching them gently with it. It is probable that it might be applied in many cases as a medicine with good effect, but I have not learnt that any experiment has been made by an inward application. It makes an excellent mouth water, and a good outward application for wounds or inflammations of every kind.

Lewis did not hesitate to try folk remedies on himself. Enroute to the Great Falls a "violent pain in the intestines" struck him during dinner the first day out and he "was unable to partake of the feast of marrowbones." He had a high fever and, traveling light, no medicines to bring it down. In desperation he resorted to a recipe his mother may have used. One of the men brought some branches from a chokeberry bush, which Lewis stripped of leaves, cut into twigs about two inches long, and boiled in a kettle of water "until a strong black decoction of an astringent bitter taste was produced." He drank a pint of the brew at sunset, another pint an hour later. "By ten in the evening I was entirely relieved from pain and in fact every symptom of the disorder forsook me. My fever abated, a gentle perspiration was produced, and I had a comfortable and refreshing night's rest." He broke fast at sunrise with another pint of his decoction and set out much relieved. (Clark had his own pharmacopoeia. Once when ill, possibly constipated, he sent Shields into the woods "to get walnut bark for pills." The next day he recorded in the journal, "my pills work.")

Lewis did not confine his practice to folk remedies. He had read in the medical literature of the day, particularly Dr. Rush's *Medical Inquiries and Observations.* When York came down with a fever, Clark gave him a dose of tartar emetic. Lewis looked on disapprovingly. "This is a description of medicine that I never have recourse to in my practice except in cases of intermittent fever." The remark could have been made by Rush, who wrote for the treatment of intermittent fever: "Begin by giving two or three grains of tartar emetic, dissolved in six tablespoons of water and one spoonful to be taken every twenty minutes, till it pukes two or three times. Work it off with warm water or any kind of weak herb tea." (Lewis had bought two pounds of tea in Philadelphia to include in his medical chest.)

Rush would also have approved of Lewis' treatment of Sacagawea. First, the captain had a man collect a cask of water from a mineral spring that streamed off a cliff across the river opposite the campsite. He had tasted the water and found it "strongly impregnated with sulpher and I suspect iron also," and it appeared to be "precisely similar to that of Bowyer's sulpher spring in Virginia," known for its medicinal virtues. Like any good physician, he kept a daily record of his patient's progress:

June 16—I found that two doses of barks and opium which I had given her since my arrival had produced an alteration in her pulse for the better; they were now much fuller and more regular. I caused her to drink the mineral water altogether. When I first came down I found that her pulse were scarcely perceptible, very quick, frequently irregular and attended with strong nervous symptoms, that of the twitching of the fingers and leaders of the arms. Now the pulse had become regular, much fuller, and a gentle perspiration had taken place. The nervous symptoms have also in a great measure abated, and she feels herself much freer from pain. She complains principally of the lower region of the abdomen. I therefore continued the cataplasms of barks and laudanum which had been previously used by my friend Capt. Clark. I believe her disorder originated principally from an obstruction of the menses in consequence of taking cold.

June 17—The Indian woman much better today. I have still continued the same course of medicine. She is free from pain, clear of fever, her pulse regular, and eats as heartily as I am willing to permit her of broiled buffalo, well seasoned with pepper and salt, and rich soup of the same meat. I think, therefore, that there is every rational hope of her recovery.

June 18—The Indian woman is recovering fast. She set up the greater part of the day and walked out for the first time since she arrived here. She eats heartily and is free from fever or pain. I continue same course of medicine and regimen except that I added one dose of fifteen drops of the oil of vitriol today about noon.

June 19—The Indian woman was much better this morning. She walked out and gathered a considerable quantity of the white apples of which she eat so heartily in their raw state, together with a considerable quantity of dried fish, without my knowledge that she complained very much and her fever again returned. I rebuked Charbonneau severely for suffering her to indulge herself with such food, he being privy to it and having been previously told what she must only eat. I now gave her broken [intermittent] doses of diluted nitre until it produced perspiration and at 10 P.M. thirty drops of laudanum which gave her a tolerable night's rest.

June 20—The Indian woman is quite free from pain and fever this morning and appears to be in a fair way for recovery. She has been walking about and fishing.

Chapter 17

The Portage

June 16, the day Lewis began ministering to Sacagawea, the party prepared to portage six bulky dugouts and thousands of pounds of baggage around five falls which, as the crow flies, stretched fifteen miles along the river. The falls were about where the Indians had said they would be; they were as impressive as predicted. Otherwise, the Indians had misled Lewis and Clark. They had said it would take no more than a half day to move around the falls, which was true for men riding horses and carrying little baggage but not true for the horseless Voyage of Discovery. They had said that the north side of the river offered the best route for a portage, but Lewis had found the north side cut by deep ravines and impossible to traverse by men loaded down with boats and provisions. Clark, upon arriving at the scene, dispatched two men to reconnoiter the south side. The end of the day brought good news and bad. Those sent to find among the scraggly trees in the neighborhood one large enough to cut wagon wheels from returned with a cottonwood twenty-two inches in diameter, probably the only one that size within twenty miles. Those sent to search for a portage route brought the bad news. "They informed us that the creek just above us and two deep ravines still higher up cut the plain between the river and mountain in such a manner that in their opinion a portage for the canoes on this side was impracticable." ("Impossible" was the word used in Clark's journal.)

"Good or bad, we must make the portage," the men were told.

Clark set out the next morning with five men to survey a path for the "impracticable" or "impossible" portage. Lewis assumed during the party's four days' absence a route would be found, and he kept the hunters busy building up a supply of meat for the time when everyone would be occupied with the portage. He ordered the white pirogue, too ponderous for even an easy portage, unloaded, pulled ashore and hidden in a thick bunch of willow bushes. The carpenters sawed several sets of wheels from the cottonwood trunk and with axletrees made from the mast of the white pirogue had soon constructed two fragile wagons. The men aired and repacked all provisions and stores. They then hauled at risk of life and limb—two of the crew were "very nearly injured essentially," that is, drowned—the six dugouts up Portage Creek, as the men called it, to a spot where the plains above were accessible.

Meanwhile, Lewis worried about the iron boat built for him at Harper's Ferry. He had the frame unpacked and assembled. It measured 36 feet long and 4½ feet in the beam. He found "all the parts complete except one screw, which the ingenuity of Shields can readily replace, a recourse which we have very frequently occasion for." He had the frame scraped clean of rust and greased. In examining the elk skins collected to cover it, he found several damaged by river water. He preferred elk over buffalo skins for the covering because he thought them stronger and less likely to shrink excessively while drying. He sent hunters out to refresh the supply. They saw plenty of deer and buffalo but no elk.

Evenings the men spent mending moccasins shredded by the

hard trip up from the Marias. One night the captain's dog Scannon disturbed the peace with constant barking, "which was unusual with him." Lewis thought there might be an Indian or grizzly lurking in the neighborhood. He sent the sergeant of the guard to investigate. "He returned soon after and reported that he believed the dog had been baying a buffalo which had attempted to swim the river just above our camp but had been beaten down by the stream, landed a little below our camp on the same side and run off."

Immense herds of buffalo were a constant presence. The mounds of their battered carcasses scattered on the banks below the falls puzzled the men for a time. They soon found an explanation. The herds had to move through narrow ravines to the river for water. Those in front were pushed by the oncoming crowd into the grip of the swift current, and some of the animals "was taken down in an instant and seen no more. Others made shore with difficulty." At times fifty or more could be seen thrashing in the river trying to make the opposite shore. "Their mangled carcasses lie along the shores below the falls in considerable quantities and afford fine amusement for the bears, wolves, and birds of prey."

The survey party returned after dark, June 20. Clark had beheld the first and greatest falls "in astonishment" but felt no need to grope for fine words to describe the sight. Instead, he set about measuring them and in the process almost slipped into the river, "at which place I must have been sucked under in an instant." From a safer perch he recorded their height at 87 feet and ¾ inches. The next day had brought another wonder, "the largest fountain or spring I ever saw, and doubt if it is not the largest in America known." On the return from the head of the falls he staked out the portage route, but darkness caught the party before more than half the path had been blazed. He figured the total portage, including the half mile up to the plains from Portage Creek, would be nearly nineteen miles. The route would be hard but passable. There were several gullies to cross plus one gradual hill and one fairly steep one.

That night the captains completed plans for the portage. Lewis with a few men would set up camp at the head of the falls and there would assemble and sheath the iron boat. Lewis continued to fret about the boat, whose ninety pounds of iron had been hauled across two-thirds of the continent. "I readily perceive several difficulties in preparing the leather boat, which are the want of convenient and proper timber, bark, skins, and above all that of pitch to pay her seams, a deficiency that I really do not know how to surmount unless it be by means of tallow and pounded charcoal, which mixture has answered a very good purpose on our wooden canoes heretofore."

The ordeal began at sunrise, June 22. The two rickety wagons carried all their brittle wheels and spindly axletrees could bear. Progress was tortuous. Prickly pears abounded everywhere and no one could avoid their spines. Herds of buffalo had trod the turf into a hard, knobby carpet "worse than frozen ground." The heaviest burden fell on those who pulled the wagons in harnesses made of elk hide. They leaned forward to catch "the grass and knobs and stones with their hands to give them more force in drawing on the canoes and loads." Sweat poured off every man, "notwithstanding the coolness of the air." At every halt, and there were many for the axletrees kept breaking, "those not employed in repairing the course, are asleep in a moment, many limping from the soreness of their feet, some become faint for a few moments."

They made eight miles by noontime. Darkness caught them still some distance from the campsite at the head of the falls. They pushed on until the tongue of one wagon gave way. Every man loaded up with all the baggage he could manage and trudged on, wincing as he trod on prickly pears hidden in the dark. They reached camp to find wolves had eaten most of the meat Clark had left there. No matter. "We soon went to sleep and slept sound."

The next morning the men back-packed in the luggage left behind the night before and then departed for the lower camp trundling the empty wagons. Clark restaked the route to shorten it by perhaps a half mile. They reached the lower camp in time to take two canoes up to the prairie and spent the evening double-soling their moccasins. Clark tried in his journal to describe the previous day's misery but gave up. "To state the fatigues of this party would take up more of the journal than other notes which I find scarcely time to set down."

Clark accompanied the men only four miles on the second portage and then, for the first and only time during the Voyage of Discovery succumbed to pain and returned to the base camp, "my feet being very sore from the walk over ruts, stones, and hills, and thro' the level plain for six days preceding, carrying my pack and gun." Later he learned that the men had endured a repeat of yesterday until in the early afternoon someone had the bright thought of raising one of the canoe's sails, "which helped us much as four men hauling at the cord with a harness." A thunderstorm caught them three miles below the upper camp. Within minutes, water inches deep lapped over their moccasins. "Our water being all gone and all the men thirsty, [we] drank hearty out of the puddles." Refreshed, they pushed on, only now through a glaze of mud that made it hard for anyone to stay upright, and "the mud stuck to the wheels in such manner that they are obliged to halt frequently and cleanse them." Still, they reached camp by dusk.

Back at the lower camp Clark awoke the next day feeling "unwell with a looseness." He treated himself to "a little coffee for breakfast, which was to me a necessity, as I had not tasted any since last winter." The men returned in the afternoon. Charbonneau, drafted as cook, served dinner, then they carried two more canoes up to the prairies. They ended the day "fatigued as usual" but still "able to shake a foot." They danced "on the green to the music of the violin which Cruzatte plays extremely well" until ten o'clock, all full of "cheerfulness and good humor."

The third portage passed with only one untoward incident. Whitehouse arrived at the upper camp "extremely ill," probably from sunstroke, though he blamed his misery on the "very hearty draught of water" he took along the way. Doctor Lewis felt his pulse, found it "full, and I therefore bled him plentifully, from which he felt great relief. I had no other instrument with which to perform this operation but my penknife; however, it answered well."

When the portage party returned to the lower camp they found Clark had lightened the remaining baggage by setting aside some of it for a new cache—Lewis' "lumbersome" desk with some of his books, his specimens of plants and animals collected since Fort Mandan; two kegs of pork, a half keg of flour, two blunderbusses, a half keg of fixed ammunition, "and some other small articles belonging to the party which could be dispensed with." Before the cache was closed Clark hoped to add his chart of the river from the mouth of the Missouri to Fort Mandan.

The provisions and other items in the cache had a significance unknown to the men. They had been meant for the canoe the captains had intended to send back to Saint Louis from this point. A number of things had led to the change in plans. The "discouraging difficulties" of the portage, totally unexpected, had made the captains uneasy about what lay ahead. The Indians had been wrong about the portage around the falls. Would they be wrong about the promised half day's portage over the Rocky Mountains? That "formidable snowy barrier" now lay dead ahead, ominous and omnipresent. Every day that Lewis and Clark looked at the soaring mountains it seemed less and less likely they could be easily surmounted. And "not having seen the Snake Indians," who had the horses needed to carry the expedition across the mountains, regardless of the ease or severity of the portage, "or knowing in fact whether to calculate on their friendship or hostility" added to the captains' uneasiness. "We also fear," Clark said, "that such a measure" of sending part of the party back to civilization "might also discourage those who would in such case remain, and might possibly hazard the fate of the expedition. We have never hinted to anyone of the party that we had such a scheme in contemplation, and all appear perfectly to have made up their minds to

Lewis's monkey flower,
discovered in August, 1805,
hand-colored engraving by
W. Hooker
LIBRARY, THE ACADEMY OF
NATURAL SCIENCES OF
PHILADELPHIA

succeed in the expedition or perish in the attempt. We all believe
that we are about to enter on the most perilous and difficult part
of our voyage, yet I see no one repining; all appear ready to meet
those difficulties which await us with resolution and becoming
fortitude."

While Cruzatte prepared the cache the men spent the afternoon carrying the last canoe and final assortment of baggage up

to the prairie. Suddenly, the sky blackened and a violent thunderstorm mixed with hail swept over them. "The hail," said Clark, "which was generally about the size of pigeon eggs and not unlike them in form, covered the ground to one inch and a half. For about twenty minutes during this storm hail fell of an enormous size, driven with violence almost incredible. When they struck the ground they would rebound to the height of ten or twelve feet and pass twenty or thirty before they touched again. During the immense storm I was with the greater part of the men on the portage. The men saved themselves, some by getting under a canoe, others by putting sundry articles on their heads. Two were knocked down and several with their legs and thighs much bruised. Capt. Lewis weighed one of those hailstones, which weighed three ounces and measured seven inches in circumference; they were generally round and solid. I am convinced if one of those had struck a man on his naked head it would certainly have fractured his skull." After the storm ended, Clark refreshed everyone with a drink of grog.

The last stage of the portage went badly from the start. Clark miscalculated the amount of baggage. It exceeded what the wagons could carry. Several barrels of pork and flour had to be left behind. The party had made only six miles when a cold rain came upon them and soaked every man through. Clark again "refreshed them with a dram," but that gave only momentary relief from a miserable night. The next day, June 29, Clark saw that the prairies were impassable for the loaded wagons. Nothing could be done until the wind and sun had dried them out. That led to a holiday for Clark and one of the few adventures he felt worth recording in the journal.

Chapter 18

A Torrent of Water

29 June 1805

A little rain very early this morning, afterwards clear. Finding that the prairie was so wet as to render it impossible to pass on to the end of the portage, determined to send back to the top of the hill at the creek for the remaining part of the baggage left at that place yesterday, leaving one man to take care of the baggage at this place. I determined myself to proceed on to the falls and take the river. According, we all set out. I took my servant and one man, Charbonneau, our interpreter, and his squaw accompanied. Soon after I arrived at the falls, I perceived a cloud which appeared black and threatened immediate rain. I looked out for a shelter but could see no place without being in great danger of being blown into the river if the wind should prove as turbulent as it is at some times. About a quarter of a mile above the falls I observed a deep ravine in which was shelving rocks, under which we took shelter near the river, and placed our guns, the compass, etc., etc., under a shelving rock on the upper side of a creek, in a place which was very secure from the rain.

The first shower was moderate, accompanied with a violent wind, the effects of which we did not feel. Soon after a torrent of rain and hail fell more violent than ever I saw before. The rain fell like one volley of water falling from the heavens and gave us time only to get out of the way of a torrent of water which was pouring down the hill into the river with immense force, tearing everything before it, taking with it large rock and mud. I took my gun and shot pouch in my left hand and with the right scrambled up the hill, pushing the interpreter's wife (who had her child in her arms) before me, the interpreter himself making attempts to pull up his wife by the hand, much scared and nearly without motion. We at length reached the top of the hill safe, where I found my servant in search of us, greatly agitated for our welfare. Before I got out of the bottom of the ravine, which was a flat dry rock when I entered it, the water was up to my waist and wet my watch. I scarcely got out before it raised ten feet deep, with a torrent which was terrible to behold, and by the time I reached the top of the hill, at least fifteen feet water.

I directed the party to return to the camp at the run as fast as possible to get to our load where clothes could be got to cover the child, whose clothes were all lost. And the woman, who was but just recovering from a severe indisposition and was wet and cold, I was fearful of a relapse. I caused her, as also the others of the party, to take a little spirits, which my servant had in a canteen, which revived them very much.

On arrival at the camp on the Willow Run met the party who had returned in great confusion to the run, leaving their loads in the plains, the hail and wind being so large and violent in the plains, and them naked, they were much bruised, and some nearly killed. One knocked down three times, and others without hats or anything on their heads bloody and complained very much. I refreshed them with a little grog. Soon after the run began to rise and rose six feet in a few minutes.

I lost at the river in the torrent the large compass, an elegant fusee, tomahawk, umbrella, shot pouch and horn with powder and ball, moccasins and the woman her child's bier and clothes, bedding, etc. The compass is a serious loss, as we have no other large one.

The plains are so wet that we can do nothing this evening, particularly as two deep ravines are between ourselves and load.

Chapter 19

The Iron Boat

After the portage party left to bring up the second load, Lewis and the men with him cleared the upper campsite of brush, chose a spot near the river under a clump of shady willows to construct his iron boat, then he handed out assignments. Frazer and Whitehouse, the party's tailors, would sew together elk skins to cover the boat. Shields and Gass would search through the thinly treed area for crossbeams—they must be straight, strong, and at least four and a half feet long—and for willow bark to line the boat. He sent out Field and Drouillard, who had returned from a fruitless search for elk along the Medicine River, to look farther up the Missouri. The boat "was a novel piece of mechanism" and Lewis must supervise every detail of the assembly. In spare moments he combed the river bank for pine driftwood from which he hoped "to obtain as much pitch as will answer to pay the seams of the boat." He also served as party cook, "in order to keep all hands employed." For his first dinner he boiled "a large quantity of excellent dried buffalo meat and made each man a large suet dumpling by way of a treat."

Compared to those in the portage party the men enjoyed light duty, flawed only by the grizzlies that cruised the area. Shields for a second time narrowly escaped being clawed to death by one. Another charged the imperturbable Drouillard, who shot it through the heart at twenty feet. Still another came one night close to camp and stole thirty pounds of buffalo suet hanging on a pole. Scannon was "in a constant state of alarm with these bear and keeps barking all night." The men routinely slept with their weapons at their side, but now Lewis made doubly sure they did, and he ordered them always to travel in pairs beyond the campsite, especially when moving through the willow brush where bears hid.

On June 27, Field and Drouillard came in with nine elk skins, but these still did not give Lewis enough to cover his boat. The next day he set Drouillard to shaving the elk skins. To speed things along he had several buffalo hides "singed pretty closely with a blazing torch," which he thought would "answer tolerable well." He waited impatiently for the portage party enroute with the last loads. He needed more hands to hasten the assembly. He expected them the evening of June 28. When they had not arrived two days later, he feared "some uncommon accident has happened." The party did not arrive until July 1, after four wretched days on the road, and not until the following day when a deposit left at six-mile stake had been retrieved could all rejoice—the portage had ended.

While Lewis fussed over his boat—the driftwood pine refused to produce pitch; the thong used to stitch the skins did not fill the needle holes "as I expected, tho' I made them sew with a large thong for that purpose"—the camp settled into a mood of relaxed tension. Some of the men dressed leather for clothing and moccasins, which "soon become rotten as they are much exposed to the water and frequently wet." Lewis asked one of the tailors to "make me some sacks of the wolf skins to transport my instruments when occasion requires their being carried any distance by land." Clark worked on his map of the Missouri from Fort Mandan to the

Great Falls. The hunters went out daily for meat to convert into pemmican, for the Indians had said to expect few buffalo after leaving the falls. The party had spent over two weeks in the vicinity of the Great Falls, yet a number of the men had not seen them. The captains arranged small sight-seeing tours.

July 4 saw the boat sheathed. It was submerged in the river to shrink the skins tight, then placed on a rack above small fires to dry her. His dream boat's appearance pleased Lewis immensely. It "completely answers my most sanguine expectation. She is not yet dry and eight men can carry her with the greatest ease. She is strong and will carry at least eight thousand pounds with her suit of hands. Her form is as complete as I could wish it." He knew the most difficult job lay ahead—"that of making her seams secure"— but felt satisfied enough to relax and join celebrating the Fourth. The party feasted on bacon, beans, suet dumplings, and buffalo meat. Lewis, once favored with dishes created by the President's French chef, relished the hump and tongue of a fat buffalo. Those "I esteem great delicacies."

Naturally, a frolic followed in the evening. "We gave the men a drink of spirits, it being the last of our stock, and some of them appeared a little sensible of its effects. The fiddle was plied and they danced very merrily until nine in the evening when a heavy shower of rain put an end to that part of the amusement." The men had no tents to sleep in—all the buffalo hides were being used to protect the baggage—and the spread sails of the canoes gave only slight cover from the rain, but nothing could dampen their spirits, and "they continued their mirth with songs and festive jokes and were extremely merry until late at night."

The next day nearly broke Lewis' heart. He awoke to see stitch holes gaping where the skins had dried tight against the boat frame. Quietly, saying nothing to Lewis, Clark told the hunters that while they scoured the countryside for game to keep their eyes open for likely trees from which to make dugouts. Meanwhile Lewis resigned himself to an expedient for caulking the boat that had worked earlier to plug cracks in the dugouts—a composition of ground charcoal, beeswax, and buffalo tallow. But first the boat had to be thoroughly dried. A thunderstorm drenched the skins "in despite of my exertions" and delayed the process a day. Finally, on July 8, all was ready. Lewis applied the composition. He stood back and reveled at his handsome creation once again. "This adds very much to her appearance, whether it will be effectual or not. It gives her hull the appearance of being formed of one solid piece. After the first coat had cooled I gave her a second which I think has made it sufficiently thick."

They launched the *Experiment*, as the men called her, on July 9. "She lay like a perfect cork on the water." Lewis ordered seats installed and the oars fitted. The six dugouts were loaded and readied for departure. Then without warning a violent wind churned the river into crashing waves. The swamped canoes were unloaded but not quickly enough; several bales of provisions were drenched. The wind pounded the party all afternoon. When it subsided the iron boat lay up to her gunwales in water. Much of the composition had peeled away "and left the seams of the boat exposed to the water and she leaked in such manner that she would not answer." During the autopsy Lewis was stunned to see that the buffalo hides had served better than those of elk. The eighth of an inch of hair he had left on them had "retained the composition perfectly and remained sound and dry." Had he only singed the elk skins instead of shaved them "I believe the composition would have remained and the boat have answered, at least until we could have reached the pine country. . . ." But too much time had been wasted for further experiments. Three months of the traveling season had been used up and the expedition had still not reached the Rocky Mountains. The party must move on. Lewis ordered the boat sunk until the skins had become soft enough to retrieve. Clark said of the set back, "this failure of our favorite boat was a great disappointment to us, we having more baggage than our canoes would carry." Lewis remarked "that this circumstance mortified me not a little," and thereafter said no more about his boat. He and Clark, indeed, all in the party, excelled at putting the past behind and moving on to whatever pain or pleasure the future held.

Now it came out that the hunters had spotted a clump of cottonwoods about eight miles up river that held a tree or two large enough for dugouts. That evening the men unpacked axes and the small grindstone that Lewis with his usual foresight had picked up in Philadelphia was put to use. The next morning Clark left with four choppers and a hunter. Lewis stayed behind to bury the iron frame, Clark's map of the Missouri and a few other papers, and the wagon wheels that had served so well and might be needed on the return trip. He dispatched loaded canoes to the new campsite. "Having nothing further to do, I amused myself fishing and caught a few small fish."

Five days passed before the two new dugouts were ready. Of the largest cottonwoods found, "one proved to be hollow and split in falling at the upper part and was somewhat windshaken at bottom; the other proved to be much windshaken." Further search turned up no better trees. Clark elected to do with what he had. He would shape the canoes "to clear the cracks and the worst of the windshaken parts, making up the deficiency by allowing them to be as wide as the trees would permit."

For some reason Clark resisted the Indian way of making a dugout—burning rather than hewing out the inside of the tree. The choppers had a miserable time. They could find no suitable wood for axehandles and broke thirteen made of chokeberry branches the first day. Mosquitoes pestered them constantly, "nor is a large black gnat less troublesome, which does not sting but attacks the eyes in swarms and compels us to brush them off or have our eyes filled with them." They worked from dawn to sunset.

They launched the canoes late in the afternoon July 14. They were fitted with seats and oars and loaded the next morning. The boats barely floated with their cargoes. A large supply of dried meat and grease, collected against the chance that game ahead would be sparse, gave the party nearly as much baggage as it had before the three caches of the past month. Also, the captains still found it "extremely difficult to keep the baggage of many of our men within reasonable bounds; they will be adding bulky articles of but little use or value to them." Until the party had eaten itself into lighter loads all non-rowers—the captains, the hunters, invalids, Charbonneau, and Sacagawea—must walk their way into the Rocky Mountains.

The canoes splashed off July 15 through a glorious setting. The prickly pear, "one of the beauties as well as the greatest pests of the plains," was in full bloom. "The sunflower is also in bloom and abundant. The lambs-quarters, wild cucumber, sand rush, and narrowdock are also common here." Ahead loomed the Rockies, the first of three visible chains of the snow-capped mountains only twenty-five miles distant.

Chapter 20

The Estimable Mr. Peale

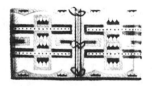

It would have cheered the captains to know that on July 13, two days before the expedition began again to paddle toward the Rocky Mountains, the first installment of the precious cargo from Fort Mandan reached President Jefferson. The shipment had been divided at Saint Louis. Clark's journal and maps and other documentary material went overland to Washington while the bulky items, including the prairie dog and birds, all still alive, rode downstream to New Orleans, where they would be loaded aboard a ship bound for Baltimore. The documentary material reached Jefferson first, shortly before he set out for his annual summer vacation at Monticello. He ignored the obvious fact that most of it came from Clark's pen. Indeed, not once in all his comments on the documents did he ever mention Clark. "We have Capt. Lewis' notes of the Missouri to his wintering place at Fort Man-

The Artist in His Museum, *painting by Charles Willson Peale*

dan," he told a friend shortly after they arrived, "and a map of the whole country watered by the Missouri and Columbia composed by himself last winter on very extensive information from Indians and traders, in which he expresses a good deal of confidence."

Jefferson was at Monticello when the rest of the cargo reached Washington on August 12. One magpie and the prairie dog had survived the four thousand-mile journey from Fort Mandan; they arrived "very well," according to Jefferson's "purveyor of the household," Etienne Lemaire. He put them "in the room where monsieur receives his callers." From Monticello Jefferson asked Lemaire to open the boxes and air the skins within. After they had been dried and brushed they should be repacked to keep them safe from the rats and mice that infested the White House. Henry Dearborn, the secretary of war, had anticipated Jefferson's uneasiness about the condition of the shipment's contents. By the time the President's instructions had reached Washington, Dearborn had seen to it that the skins in boxes, which he suspected would be rife with vermin, had been hung for four days in the sun, then repacked in linen sacks with a layer of leaf tobacco to deter further inroads by small but noxious animals.

Jefferson returned to Washington early in October to face a problem largely of his own making—what should the President do with the treasures Captains Lewis and Clark had shipped back? The federal government had financed the Voyage of Discovery. It owned everything that materialized from the expedition. The War Department was equipped to handle the maps and reports of the captains, but what about the specimens of flora and fauna, the samples of minerals and soils, the Indian artifacts? The federal government had no museums to display these things nor scientists on the payroll to study them, and with Jefferson's strict interpretation of the Constitution it never would. What, then, should be done with the cargo from Fort Mandan?

Jefferson gave a partial answer to the question by appropriating for his own pleasure and amusement several of the items for himself. He was planning an Indian Hall for the lobby at Monticello,

Mandan Buffalo Robe, similar to the one sent by Lewis and Clark to
Thomas Jefferson, aquatint of watercolor by Karl Bodmer

and the Mandan bow with its quiver of arrows, the earthen pot, one of the buffalo robes, some articles of Indian dress, the horns of a wapiti and of a bighorn sheep—neither of which had been seen in the East or was known to science—would fit nicely into the display. Jefferson dispatched the rest of the shipment to Philadelphia. A selection of the seeds sent back by Lewis went to William Hamilton, whose estate on the edge of Philadelphia was studded with gardens that for their collections of foreign and native plants, their taste and style, were, said Jefferson, "the only rival which I have known in America to what may be seen in England." The sixty-seven specimens of soils, minerals, and salts and the sixty specimens of pressed plants went to the American Philosophical Society with the understanding that Dr. Benjamin Smith Barton be allowed free access to the collections in order to identify them for the scientific world. The rest of the cargo— the skins and occasional skeletons of the weasel, coyote, jack rabbit, red fox, grizzly bear, badger, and antelope, along with the flourishing magpie and prairie dog—went to Charles Willson Peale, proprietor and creator of what was at the time the greatest museum in the western world.

Peale was one of the luckiest things that happened to the Voyage of Discovery. Through him and the care he lavished on the shipment from Fort Mandan, every item of which he soon had artfully displayed in his museum, the public became aware of a host of animals then unknown to science. Jefferson's instructions had set the tone for the expedition, but it was Peale—the estimable Mr. Peale—who, almost singlehanded, let the world know the Voyage was more than a mere exploratory trek through the wilderness.

Excepting John Singleton Copley and Benjamin West, both of whom lived and painted in London, Peale was the foremost American artist of his day. The sales of his paintings fed and clothed his huge brood of children—eleven by his first wife, six by his second, none, for some reason, by his third, unless it be that she, like he, was well into the seventh decade—but by the end of the Revolution he was looking for other ways to occupy his restless mind. An interest in natural history led him in 1784 to open a museum in his home as an adjunct to his portrait gallery of Revolutionary leaders, to which he had long charged admission. By 1805, when Jefferson sent him the shipment from Fort Mandan, the museum had expanded from Peale's home to the American Philosophical Society's Hall, to, finally, the State House, where it occupied the second and third floors and the brick-walled yard behind, which housed a bald eagle, an orang-utang, two grizzly bears, several monkeys, and a number of other animals in Peale's menagerie.

Peale's Museum was unique. Unlike the British Museum in London and the National Museum in Paris, it was self-supporting. Indeed, it made money—nearly $5,000 in 1805, a large sum then, and increasingly more in the years that followed—and eventually netted Peale a small fortune. It was unique, too, in that instead of offering a hodgepodge of disparate displays, as its European counterparts did, Peale fitted each of his into the scientific order of the Linnean system of classification. He wanted to "bring into view a world in miniature." What further set his museum apart and put it at least a half century ahead of its time was the way Peale presented his specimens. Each received the care and attention he devoted to a painting. He was a self-taught but skillful taxidermist. (A century later an ornithologist said, "it is quite easy to recognize C.W. Peale's birds by their fine condition. He was a good taxidermist.") He shaped every specimen into a natural pose and then placed it in something approximate to its natural habitat. From a thicket of trees a visitor might see peeping out a bear, a raccoon, or a wildcat. The boughs of the trees were weighed down with birds. In a nearby artificial pond would be a "collection of fish with their skins stuffed," and scattered on the beach around the pond a variety of "water fowls, such as the different species of geese, ducks, cranes, herons, etc., all having the appearance of life. . . ." In another exhibit he placed the head of a rattlesnake under a magnifying glass, so arranged that the visitor could clearly see every detail of the fangs and the poison ducts.

Peale hoped that some day the federal government would allow him to bequeath his museum to the nation. "At my time of life I cannot help feeling some anxiety to know the fate of my labors," he told Jefferson. "Everything I do is with a view of a permanency, yet at my death there is a danger of its being divided or lost to my country." Jefferson could give him no aid or comfort, for as he read the Constitution the federal government had no more right to countenance a museum than it did a national bank. (And so the museum was lost forever to its country.) But it did have the right, as Jefferson saw it, to turn over to Peale's Museum the skins and skeletons and live animals sent back by Lewis and Clark. Jefferson did not make clear whether he, as President, gave these items to Peale or merely loaned them to him, using the museum as a temporary depository. If they were on loan, then they must be returned to the government if Peale's Museum ceased to exist. The question was academic, or so Jefferson treated it—unfortunately. The President's failure to deal with it contributed in the long run to the tragedy of the Voyage of Discovery. Jefferson knew that Charles Willson Peale was an honorable, an estimable man. The shipment from Fort Mandan could not be in better hands. That was enough for Thomas Jefferson.

The shipment reached Peale's Museum late in October. Peale told the President at once of its arrival and a week and a half later sent along his first progress report. "The skeletons are much broken," he said, "and I fear some of the bones are lost at the places where they have been opened. I can mend the broken bones but cannot make good the deficiency of lost bones. Being mixed together is of no great consequence, as every bone must find its fellow bone. Whether I can get an entire skeleton from all this mass of bones, I cannot yet determine. It will be a work of time and exercise of much patience. This I shall not regard, provided the object is accomplished and the loss of bones will be my only obstacle in the work. I wish the skeletons had not been mixed with the skins, for the uncleaned bones bred the insects which afterwards fed on the skins and has entirely destroyed some of them."

By the end of the year Peale had pieced together the skeleton of an antelope and fitted one of the ratty skins over the frame. The skins had been so ravaged by vermin, he told Jefferson, "that it was with much difficulty I could mount one of them, but being so interesting an animal, I conceived it was better to have one even in bad condition than to let it be wanting in the museum. . . ." To help publicize Lewis and Clark's discovery of an animal hitherto unknown to science, Peale prepared a drawing for the American Philosophical Society's *Transactions*. Lewis had called the animal an antelope, which up to now had been found only in Africa and Asia. Jefferson, after studying "the bony prominence to the cranium on which the horn is fixed," came to agree with Lewis. He felt this proved "that the animal is of the antelope family." Peale, hesitantly, reached a different conclusion. He could not fit to satisfaction the specimen in his museum workshop into Linnaeus' classification of antelope. What, then, a member of the

American Philosophical Society asked, would he call the animal? "The forked horned antelope," Peale said after a moment's reflection. "But, sir," he wrote Jefferson after the meeting, "that is not a scientific name. It is not a Latin name but one most descriptive of the animal, since we know of no antelope besides having forked horns." He urged the President to give the beast a formal name or else find out what the Indians called it and use that name to identify the mysterious animal. Scientists ever since have been saddened that Jefferson did not listen to Peale's plea. "This beautiful creature," Paul Russell Cutright has recently written, "is of course, not an antelope at all, and in fact has no close relative anywhere in the world. To find a correct taxonomic niche for it, scientists had to create an entirely new family (*Antilocapridae*), which it has all to itself. It is the only mammal having a hollow horn that is branched and that is shed and renewed each year."

While Peale was reconstructing the antelope skeleton, Dr. Benjamin Smith Barton visited the museum to study the magpie and prairie dog, both of which were thriving on Peale's solicitous care. Barton identified the magpie correctly as "unquestionably" of the *Corvus* species, an opinion every knowledgeable person who had seen the bird had reached earlier. The marmot, as Barton and all who saw the prairie dog called it, "I take . . . to be the *Arctomys citillus*, common in the north of Asia." Here Barton was dead wrong, but a decade passed before the squirrel-like animal received its correct Latin binomial, *Cynomys ludovicianus lucovicianus*. Barton's comments on the fauna returned from Fort Mandan mattered little, for his specialty was botany. Jefferson awaited Barton's professional opinion on the sixty pressed plants Lewis had sent back. Among colleagues, Barton was generally known as a man slow to deliver on promises, but Jefferson could only have been pleased when the doctor announced, soon after riffling through Lewis' specimens, that he was preparing a catalogue of the plants the captain had collected which "would serve as a beginning of a *Flora Missourica*."

It would have pleased Lewis and Clark to have known while

they still paddled toward the Pacific how well the President—his gifts to himself aside—had handled the first shipment from the wilderness. Peale's displays in the museum had already put before the world the new animals they had discovered and Barton had promised soon to do the same for the new plants they had uncovered. Under Jefferson's direction the cartographer Nicholas King had reduced Clark's map of the Missouri Valley to manageable proportions; an engraving had been made from his copy which the War Department was ready to distribute. After a close study of Clark's chart and Lewis's essay on the tribes living in the Missouri Valley, Jefferson prepared an essay entitled "A statistical view . . . of the Indian nations inhabiting the territory of Louisiana and the countries adjacent to its northern and western borders, of their commerce, and of other interesting circumstances respecting them." The essay was a "pioneering classic" in the ethnology of western Indians. Tribes hitherto shadowy names only—the Kansas, Oto, Arikara, Sioux—now became clearly delineated. Jefferson felt free to have it printed at government expense because, obliquely at least, it dealt with commerce, a matter the Constitution judged of federal concern. By allowing the paper to come out under the government's imprimateur Jefferson established, to his chagrin, a precedent that soon led to federal publication of many reports of expeditions financed by the government. But what concerned Jefferson at the end of 1805 was, regardless of what the Constitution said or what the President thought it said, to get the findings of the Voyage of Discovery into the mainstream of western thought. Peale was doing that through his museum and so, soon, would Barton do. Jefferson at the time and for some years afterward was unaware he had been deluded by the glib tongue and earnest promises of Dr. Benjamin Smith Barton.

Chapter 21

In Search of Indians

The next landmark the party headed for lay some two hundred miles ahead, where the Indians at Fort Mandan had told them the Missouri branched into three forks. The expedition should take the northern one of the three, which would carry it to the feet of mountains on the other side of which lay the Columbia River. The party would need horses to cross the mountains, and from the day the boats shoved off on this new leg of the journey everyone kept alert for signs of the Snake Indians, known for their numerous and fine steeds. Lewis had already found evidence that they, or other mounted Indians, had recently roamed the neighborhood. While waiting for the dugouts to be finished he had stumbled on an extraordinary lodge. Not its shape, that of a typical conical tepee, but its size struck him. The lodge poles were cottonwood trunks fifty feet long. The circumference of the lodge's base was 216 feet. "I never saw a similar one nor do the nations lower down the Missouri construct such."

The second day on the river revealed more Indian cultural spoor—"about forty little booths formed of willow bushes to shelter them from the sun. They appeared to have been deserted about ten days. We supposed that they were Snake Indians. They appeared to have a number of horses with them. Their appearance gives me much hope of meeting with these people shortly."

On July 17, the boats nosed into a canyon and mild rapids riffled the hitherto smooth river. Along the tops of the cliffs they saw some bighorn sheep, an animal they had heard about back in Saint Louis and from whose scooped-out horns they had eaten when among the Teton Sioux. The hunters tried but failed to bring one down. "On the face of this cliff they walked about and bounded from rock to rock with apparent unconcern where it appeared to me that no quadruped could have stood and from which had they made one false step they must have been precipitated at least five hundred feet. This animal appears to frequent such precipices and cliffs where in fact they are perfectly secure from the pursuit of the wolf, bear, or even man himself."

The next day a "handsome, bold, and clear stream" cut into the Missouri from the north. They named it Dearborn River, after the secretary of war. The Indians had told them that this river offered a short cut through the Rocky Mountains. But Jefferson had instructed Lewis to follow the Missouri to its source. Also, the party needed horses more than a shortcut. Clark, taking Joseph Field, Potts, and York with him, left the river at the Dearborn to search out the Snakes. He feared that "the daily discharge of our guns [might] alarm and cause them to retreat to the mountains and conceal themselves."

The day the captains separated they traveled in different worlds. Clark's party in the mountains dined on elk meat and venison while those in the boats feasted on otter and beaver dragged from the river. Firewood abounded in the river bottoms, but Clark, in the treeless hills, had to resort to buffalo chips—dried dung—which he had seen Indians on the plains use. They shared only the ubiquitous prickly pear. The first night out Clark pulled

Bighorn, discovered April 26, 1805, engraving by Alexander Lawson

seventeen briars from his swollen feet by the light of the fire of chips. Those walking the river bank fared little better.

The boats, on July 19, rowed through a portal of cliffs so impressive that Lewis called them *The Gates of the Rocky Mountains*. "These cliffs rise from the water's edge on either side perpendicularly to the height of 1,200 feet. Every object here wears a dark and gloomy aspect. The towering and projecting rocks in many places seem ready to tumble on us. The river appears to have forced its way through this immense body of solid rock for the distance of five and three-quarters miles, and where it makes its exit below has thrown on either side vast columns of rocks mountains high. The river appears to have worn a passage just the width of its channel or 150 yards. It is deep from side to side, nor is there in the first three miles of this distance a spot, except one of a few yards in extent, on which a man could rest the sole of his foot. Several fine springs burst out at the water's edge from the interstices of the rocks. It happens, fortunately, that altho' the current is strong it is not so much so but what it may be overcome

The Gate of the Mountains, discovered in mid-July, 1805,
pencil sketch by A.E. Mathews

with the oars, for there is here no possibility of using either the cord or setting pole." The boats had to travel some distance after dark to find a decent camping spot. The pitch pine Lewis had wanted so desperately a few days ago abounded around the campsite.

Mid-morning the next day the river party saw smoke rise, "as if the country had been set on fire." All hearts sank. The expedition knew that Indians set the plains on fire as a warning sign to all tribes that an enemy approached. The Snakes must now be laboriously flushed from their mountain retreats.

The boats pushed on into a wide, fertile valley where the river, no longer cramped by rock walls, spread to more than a mile in width. Sacagawea recognized the spot and said "that this is the river on which her relations live, and that the Three Forks are at no great distance." This news "cheered the spirits of the party, who now begin to console themselves with the anticipation of shortly seeing the head of the Missouri, yet unknown to the civilized world." Sacagawea, whose tribe lived principally on roots, probably guided Lewis to an island blanketed with "crisp and well-flavored" wild onions. He called a halt for breakfast and let the men gather enough to snack on through the day.

They came upon Clark toward the end of the valley in the afternoon, sitting on the bank nursing swollen feet. He had seen the remains of several Indian camps, some only a few days old. He had left pieces of tape, paper, and linen on bushes along his trail as a sign he came as a friend. He knew he had been spotted but was determined to push on with the search, although he could not take a step without wincing. Lewis tried to dissaude him, but with a stubbornness not usual with him Clark refused to give up the chase. "Finding him anxious," said Lewis, "I readily consented to remain with the canoes."

The first day out Clark, with Frazer, the Field brothers, and Charbonneau, traveled twenty-five miles over an Indian road. On the third day, July 25, they reached the Three Forks. Horse tracks in the vicinity were only four or five days old. Clark left a note for

Left, Western tanager and Right, Lewis's woodpecker, discovered June 6, 1806, and July 20, 1805, by Lewis. Center, Clark's nutcracker afterwards called Clark's crow, discovered August 22, 1805, by Clark. Hand-colored engravings from Alexander Wilson's ornithology.

the boat party saying he would explore the western fork, which the Indians at Fort Mandan had said led into the mountains. After another twenty-five-mile hike the feet of Joseph Field and Charbonneau gave out. Clark's, too, were lacerated, but he pushed ahead and up a mountain for a view of the country. The fork he had been traveling continued meandering westward, just as the Indians had said it would. Back in camp Clark felt too sick to eat—he blamed the illness on drinking "excessively" from an ice cold mountain stream—and although "fatigued, my feet with several blisters, and stuck with *prickly pears*," he refused to rest. The party pushed on to explore the middle fork. That night he had a high fever, frequent chills, and ached in every bone, yet the next day he traveled up the middle fork. By nightfall he felt "very unwell, fever very high." He thought himself "somewhat bilious" and since he had not "had a passage for several days" took five of Dr. Rush's thunderbolts, then bathed his feet in a kettle of warm water.

The boats reached the forks on July 27. The men had suffered up the twisting, rapid river. Occasionally, to relieve a man Lewis had joined "in the labor of navigating the canoes and have learned to *push a tolerable good pole* in their phrase." They had found a new pest to add to a growing list—a needle-like grass armed with a hard beard and stiff bristles sharp enough to "answer as a barb," penetrate moccasins, and give "great pain." Scannon suffered "with them excessively."

Both captains saw instantly that the forks offered a fine spot for a fort or trading post. Here the country opened "to extensive and beautiful plains and meadows" ringed by the still distant but soaring mountains. They named the first two of the "noble streams" that joined to form the Missouri after Albert Gallatin and James Madison and the third, which they judged the main one, after the noblest of them all, Thomas Jefferson. On this spot Sacagawea had been captured five years earlier. She showed no sign of sorrow or "of joy in being again restored to her native country." Her reaction chilled Lewis: "If she has enough to eat and a few trinkets to wear I believe she would be perfectly content anywhere."

Despite everyone's eagerness to make contact with the Snakes, the party paused for three leisurely days at the forks. Lewis wanted to make celestial observations; Clark was too ill to move—the men built a bower to shade him from the sun—the baggage needed to be aired and dried; and all the crew needed a rest. Clark's fever soon dropped but he still felt weak and languid. Lewis persuaded him to take a dose of bark, "which he has done and eat tolerably freely of our good venison." Once again a mood of relaxed tension pervaded the camp.

If we do not find them or some other nation who have horses I fear the successful issue of our voyage will be very doubtful, or at all events much more difficult in its accomplishment. We are now several hundred miles within the bosom of this wild and mountainous country, where game may rationally be expected shortly to become scarce and subsistence precarious without any information with respect to the country, not knowing how far these mountains continue, or where to direct our course to pass them to advantage or intercept a navigable branch of the Columbia, or even were we on such an one the probability is that we should not find any timber within these mountains large enough for canoes if we judge from the portion of them through which we have passed. However, I still hope for the best.

The Jefferson's westward course consoled them—it must "head with the waters of . . . the Columbia"—and the thought that "if any Indians can subsist in the form of a nation in these mountains with the means they have of acquiring food we can also subsist."

The party's morale had now dipped to the lowest since the trip began. The narrow, twisting, still rapid but barely navigable river made the boatsmen's lives a daily hell. For the first time they lacked fresh meat and had to draw on provisions brought from Saint Louis. And they had barely entered the mountains. Clark, still weak, had to abdicate his role of scout to Lewis, who the next day, August 1, left with Drouillard, Gass, and Charbonneau. Before leaving he took a dose of Glauber's salts to clean his system of a mild attack of dysentery. He had to stop several times during the morning to relieve himself and after a hike through the hills regained the river exhausted. He dined on one of the elks he and Drouillard had shot and felt better. They left what meat remained on a pole for the party coming up, which had "had no fresh meat for near two days." The lowering Jefferson, now shallow enough to wade, told them what the men below endured, that they were being "obliged to drag the canoes over the stones, there not being enough water to float them."

On August 4, Lewis came to a spot where the Jefferson forked into three branches. He explored them all, left a note on a stick—take the middle branch—then pushed on to double-check the course of that stream. Convinced it entered the range of mountains ahead, he returned downstream to a disconsolate scene. Clark had an inflamed swelling on his ankle and could barely walk. The canoes had taken the wrong branch because Lewis had put his note on a green stick which a beaver came up and ate. The river had swamped two canoes and drenched their cargoes and a third canoe had overset and nearly drowned one man, who, if the water had been two inches shallower would have been crushed to death as the boat swung over him. "Our parched meal, corn, Indian presents, and a great part of our most valuable stores were wet and much damaged on this occasion." The lead canisters of powder had survived hours under water but a wooden keg holding twenty pounds of powder had leaked and spoiled the contents. Atop all this Shannon was lost again.

This, perhaps the most critical day since the expedition began, both Lewis and Clark described fully but quietly in their journals. They had only a month's traveling time, if that, to get through the Rocky Mountains. They had seen no recent signs of the Snake Indians. Yet no hint of anxiety appears in the entries. Lewis ends his saying that he and Clark had "determined that the middle fork was that which ought of right to bear the name we had given to the lower portion or *River Jefferson*, and called the bold, rapid, and clear stream *Wisdom* [Big Hole, today], and the more mild and placid one which flows in from the southeast *Philanthropy*, in commemoration of two of those cardinal virtues which have so eminently marked that deservedly celebrated character through life."

Chapter 22

Indians!

It took a day to dry the stores. In reloading them the captains saw that enough had been lost or used up to dispense with a canoe. The men hid it in a thicket of brush. Lewis tinkered with his air gun, which he wanted in working order to impress the Indians. On August 8, the canoes started again up the river. The party passed a point Sacagawea said her people called Beaver's Head. Their summer camp was not "very distant," she said. This news and signs that the river would soon be unnavigable—it had shrunk to a width of twenty-five yards, was seldom more than ten feet deep, and very crooked—convinced Lewis he must set out again to find the Indians. Clark's swollen ankle "discharged a considerable amount of matter" that day but he could still walk, barely.

Lewis rose with the sun next day, left camp alone, and found a spot along the river a few miles upstream. "By this means I acquired leisure to accomplish some writings which I conceived from the nature of my instructions necessary lest any accident should

befall me on the long and rather hazardous route I was now about
to take." With the journal up to date he returned to breakfast with
the party. Shannon showed up during the meal. He had been gone
three days, "had lived very plentifully this trip but looked a good
deal worried with his march."

After breakfast Lewis prepared to take up again the search for
Indians. From Sacagawea he got what he thought were the Snake
words for "white man"—*tab-ba-bone*. He chose his usual pair to
travel with him—Drouillard and Shields—and McNeal to act as
cook. They carried some flour, parched meal, and pork to subsist
on if game proved scarce. Lewis packed some small American
flags and an assortment of trinkets. Clark watched the departure
with envy. But for "the raging fury of a tumor on my ankle
muscle," he said, "I should have taken this trip."

The search group made sixteen miles the first day. Every time
they struck the river—"very crooked, much divided by islands,
shallow, rocky in many places, and very rapid"—they felt for those
coming up it, "insomuch that I have my doubts whether the
canoes could get on or not; or if they do, it must be with great
labor."

The next day they fell in with an Indian road which led
toward a point where the river appeared to emerge from hills to
the west. They dined in the shadow of "an immensely high,
perpendicular" rock wall that Lewis called Rattlesnake Cliffs.
(Here Clark was twice almost bitten and once while fishing looked
down to see a rattler curled between his spread feet.) Fifteen
miles later "we arrived in a handsome open and level valley where
the river divided itself nearly into two equal branches." Lewis knew
that after some three thousand miles on the Missouri the canoes
must at last be beached. No canoe could pass beyond this fork.
He left a note to Clark on a *dry* willow stick to halt the expedition
here and await his return.

The next day brought into view an Indian mounted on a fine
horse. The excited Lewis dropped his pocket telescope, yanked a
blanket from his knapsack and holding it by the corners waved it

three times in the air then spread it on the ground. Among the Plains Indians this was a universal sign of welcome. The Indian kept his distance. Lewis signalled Drouillard and Shields, some distance on his flanks, to cease moving ahead. He raged inwardly when neither had "sagacity enough to recollect the impropriety of advancing when they saw me thus in parley with the Indian." Drouillard caught the signal, stopped, put down his gun. Shields missed it, and as he continued to move up the Indian eyed him suspiciously. Lewis dangled trinkets in the air. He left his gun and powder pouch with McNeal and walked slowly ahead. At two hundred paces the Indian backed off. Lewis shouted *tab-ba-bone* several times. He paused to strip back his shirt sleeve and show the white skin of his arm. At a hundred yards the Indian gave his horse the whip and vanished in the willow brush. "I now called the men to me and could not forebear abrading them a little for their want of attention and imprudence on this occasion."

They followed the Indian's tracks toward the line of hills to the north. Lewis feared his party was being watched from the hills and that any suspicious move would send the Indians further into the mountains. "I therefore halted in an elevated situation near the creek, had a fire kindled of willow brush, cooked and took breakfast." He hung moccasin awls, beads, vermillion, a looking glass, and other trinkets on a pole and then resumed the march, with McNeal now carrying the American flag on a stick. Rain obliterated the Indian's tracks. They camped near the stream they had been following and planted the flag pole close to their fire.

The next day in mid-morning they came upon a much used Indian road that paralleled the stream. Soon both "swung abruptly to the west through a narrow bottom between the mountains." A few miles further the stream diminished to a rivulet trickling down the hillside. McNeal, with the flag in hand and "exulting, stood with a foot on each side of this little rivulet and thanked his God that he had lived to bestride the mighty and heretofore deemed endless Missouri." Further up the hill everyone paused to drink from this "most distant fountain of the waters of the mighty Missouri, in search of which we have spent so many toil-some days and restless nights."

They moved over the "dividing ridge"—the Continental Di-vide—and on the western slope saw "a handsome running creek of cold, clear water." "Here," said Lewis, "I first tasted the water of the great Columbia River." The view muted his joy. From the hillside he saw "immense ranges of high mountains still to the west of us with their tops partially covered with snow." If the stream he had just drunk from merged with others into a navigable river that went through or around those mountains all would be well. If it did not, all would be hell.

They continued down the Indian road until sunset, camped, and boiled the last of their pork, for they had killed no game all day. They had only a little flour and parched meal left. They were off again at sunrise following the twisting, dusty road through mountain valleys. Mid-morning they spied about a mile ahead two women, a man, and some dogs on a rise. The Indians sat down, "as if to await our arrival." Lewis dropped his rifle, took the flag, and advanced slowly. The women vanished but the man waited until Lewis was within a hundred yards "and then likewise ab-sconded." The dogs, however, stayed. Lewis tried to use them as messengers by tying a bright-colored handkerchief with some beads and trinkets about their necks, but the dogs likewise absconded.

Lewis knew that the village that must be nearby would soon be warned of his party's presence. He quickened the pace down the road. A mile later they came suddenly upon two girls and an old woman. One girl scampered away but the other two, too close to run, stayed put, seating "themselves on the ground, holding down their heads as if reconciled to die." Lewis lifted them up and once more went through his routine—laid down his gun, said *tab-ba-bone* several times, stripped back his sleeve and pointed at his white skin, and dangled trinkets before them. Through Drouillard, who was fluent in sign language, he asked the old lady to call back the girl who had raced away. She did, and the girl quickly came up, still puffing from her run. Lewis painted the face of each with vermillion, a symbol of peace Sacagawea had said. He asked to be taken to their chief.

Two miles down the road the party saw some sixty warriors armed for battle galloping toward them. The Indians reined up and their chief came forward to talk to the women. They showed off their presents. The chief signalled that the strangers were friends. The Indians "now advanced and we were all caressed and besmeared with their grease and paint till I was heartily tired of the national hug." There on the road the Indians sat in a circle and after pulling off their moccasins smoked the pipe of peace. Lewis passed out trinkets and gave the flag to the chief "as the bond of union between us." All now moved down the road to the village four miles ahead. They arrived to find that a vanguard of warriors had prepared a willow brush lodge and a tepee for their guests. The pipe-smoking ceremony was repeated, only this time the white men were told they, too, should take off their moccasins—a ritual which meant that in this land of the prickly pear a man must hereafter go barefoot if his profession of friendship was not sincere. By now it was late in the afternoon. None of Lewis' party had eaten since the previous night. The chief said he had nothing to offer but "some cakes of serviceberries and chokeberries which had been dried in the sun." These were welcomed.

After the scanty meal Lewis asked about the stream that ran past the village. The chief, whose name was Cameahwait, said it discharged itself into another as large at the distance of a half day's march, but this second river, the Salmon, was very rapid and rocky and "it was impossible for us to pass either by land or water down this river to the great lake where the white men lived." Another Indian helped offset this depressing news when he offered Lewis a piece of freshly roasted salmon. This "perfectly convinced me that we were on the waters of the Pacific Ocean." Drouillard came in from a tour of the village to say the tribe had some four hundred excellent horses. Lewis went to look them over. "Indeed, many of them would make a figure on the south side of the James River, or the land of fine horses."

The Indians had a frolic that night that lasted nearly to dawn. Lewis went to bed at midnight, "leaving the men to amuse themselves with the Indians." Several times during the night he was awakened "by their yells but was too much fatigued to be deprived of a tolerable sound night's repose."

Chapter 23

"I Arose Hungry as a Wolf"

15 August 1805

This morning I arose very early and as hungry as a wolf. I had
eaten nothing yesterday except one scant meal of the flour and
berries (except the [Indians'] dried cakes of berries, which did not
appear to satisfy my appetite as they appeared to do those of my
Indian friends). I found on inquiry of McNeal that we had only
about two pounds of flour remaining. This I directed him to divide
into two equal parts and to cook the one half this morning in a
kind of pudding with the berries as he had done yesterday and
reserve the balance for the evening. On this new-fashioned pudding
four of us breakfasted, giving a pretty good allowance also to the
chief, who declared it the best thing he had tasted for a long time.
He took a little of the flour in his hand, tasted and examined it
very scrutinously and asked me if we made it of roots. I explained
to him the manner in which it grew.

I hurried the departure of the Indians. The chief addressed

them several times before they would move. They seemed very reluctant to accompany me. I at length asked the reason and he told me that some foolish persons among them had suggested the idea that we were in league with the Pahkees [Blackfeet] and had come on in order to decoy them into an ambuscade where their enemies were waiting to receive them. But that for his part he did not believe it. I readily perceived that our situation was not entirely free from danger, as the transition from suspicion to the confirmation of the fact would not be very difficult in the minds of these ignorant people who have been accustomed from their infancy to view every stranger as an enemy. I told Cameahwait that I was sorry to find that they had put so little confidence in us, that I knew they were not acquainted with white men and therefore could forgive them. That among white men it was considered disgraceful to lie or entrap an enemy by falsehood. I told him if they continued to think thus meanly of us that they might rely on it that no white men would ever come to trade with them or bring them arms and ammunition, and that if the bulk of his nation still entertained this opinion I still hoped that there were some among them that were not afraid to die, that [they] were men and would go with me and convince themselves of the truth of what I had asserted. That there was a party of white men waiting my return either at the forks of Jefferson River or a little below, coming on to that place in canoes loaded with provisions and merchandise. He told me for his own part he was determined to go, that he was not afraid to die.

I soon found that I had touched him on the right string. To doubt the bravery of a savage is at once to put him on his metal. He now mounted his horse and harangued his village a third time. The purport of which, as he afterwards told me, was to inform them that he would go with us and convince himself of the truth or falsity of what we had told him. . . . He hoped there were some of them who heard him were not afraid to die with him, and if there were to let him see them mount their horses and prepare to set out.

Shortly after this harangue he was joined by six or eight only, and with these I smoked a pipe and directed the men to put on their packs, being determined to set out with them while I had them in the humor. At half past twelve we set out. Several of the old women were crying and imploring the Great Spirit to protect their warriors as if they were going to inevitable destruction. We had not proceeded far before our party was augmented by ten or twelve more and before we reached the creek which we had passed in the morning of the 13th it appeared to me that we had all the men of the village and a number of the women with us. This may serve in some measure to illustrate the capricious disposition of those people, who never act but from the impulse of the moment. They were now very cheerful and gay, and two hours ago they looked as surly as so many imps of Saturn.

When we arrived at the spring on the side of the mountain where we had encamped on the 12th, the chief insisted on halting to let the horses graze, with which I complied and gave the Indians a smoke. They are excessively fond of the pipe, but have it not much in their power to indulge themselves with even their native tobacco as they do not cultivate it themselves. After remaining about an hour, we again set out, and, by engaging to make compensation to four of them for their trouble, [we each] obtained the privilege of riding with an Indian. . . . I soon found it more tiresome riding without stirrups than walking and of course chose the latter, making the Indian carry my pack.

About sunset we reached the upper part of the level valley of the cove which we now called Shoshoni Cove. The grass being burned on the north side of the river, we passed over to the south and encamped near some willow brush about four miles above the narrow pass between the hills noticed as I came up this cove. The river here was about six yards wide, and frequently dammed up by the beaver. I had sent Drouillard forward this evening before we halted to kill some meat, but he was unsuccessful and did not rejoin us until after dark. I now cooked and divided among six of us to eat the remaining pound of flour stirred in a little boiling water.

16 August 1805

I sent Drouillard and Shields before this morning in order to kill some meat, as neither the Indians nor ourselves had anything to eat. I informed the chief of my view in this measure and requested that he would keep his young men with us lest by their hooping and noise they should alarm the game and we should get nothing to eat. But so strongly were their suspicions excited by this measure that two parties of discovery immediately set out, one on each side of the valley, to watch·the hunters, as I believe, to see whether they had not been sent to give information of their approach to an enemy that they still persuaded themselves were lying in wait for them. I saw that any further effort to prevent their going would only add strength to their suspicions and therefore said no more.

After the hunters had been gone about an hour we set out. We had just passed through the narrows when we saw one of the spies coming up the level plain under whip. The chief paused a little and seemed somewhat concerned. I felt a good deal so myself and began to suspect that by some unfortunate accident that perhaps some of their enemies had straggled hither at this unlucky moment. But we were all agreeably disappointed on the arrival of the young man to learn that he had come to inform us that one of the white men had killed a deer. In an instant they all gave their horses the whip and I was taken nearly a mile before I could learn what were the tidings. As I was without stirrups and an Indian behind me, the jostling was disagreeable. I therefore reined up my horse and forbid the Indian to whip him, who had given him the lash at every jump for a mile, fearing he should lose part of the feast. The fellow was so uneasy that he left me the horse, dismounted and ran on foot at full speed I am confident a mile.

When they arrived where the deer was, which was in full view of me, they dismounted and ran in tumbling over each other like a parcel of famished dogs, each seizing and tearing away a part of the intestines which had been previously thrown out by Drouillard, who killed it. The scene was such when I arrived that had I not have had a pretty keen appetite myself I am confident I should not have tasted any part of the venison shortly. Each one had a piece of some description and all eating most ravenously. Some were eating the kidneys, the milt, and liver, and the blood running from the corners of their mouths; others were in a similar situation with the paunch and guts, but the exuding substance in this case from their lips was of a different description. One of the last who attracted my attention particularly had been fortunate in his allotment, or rather active in his division; he had provided himself with about nine feet of the small guts, one end of which he was chewing on while with his hands he was squeezing the contents out at the other. I really did not until now think that human nature ever presented itself in a shape so nearly allied to the brute creation. I viewed those poor starved devils with pity and compassion. I directed McNeal to skin the deer and reserved a quarter; the balance I gave the chief to be divided among his people. They devoured the whole of it nearly without cooking.

I now bore obliquely to the left in order to intercept the creek where there was some brush to make a fire and arrived at this stream where Drouillard had killed a second deer. Here nearly the same scene was enacted. A fire being kindled we cooked and eat and gave the balance of the two deer to the Indians who eat the whole of them, even to the soft parts of the hoofs. Drouillard joined us at breakfast with a third deer. Of this I reserved a quarter and gave the balance to the Indians. They all appeared now to have filled themselves and were in good humor.

This morning early, soon after the hunters set out, a considerable part of our escort became alarmed and returned; twenty-eight men and three women only continued with us.

After eating and suffering the horses to graze about two hours

*Lewis wearing the tippet
presented by a Shoshoni
chief, watercolor by Charles
de Saint-Memin*
COURTESY NEW-YORK HISTORICAL
SOCIETY

we renewed our march and towards evening arrived at the lower
part of the cove. Shields killed an antelope on the way, a part of
which we took and gave the remainder to the Indians.

Being now informed of the place at which I expected to meet
Capt. C. and the party, they insisted on making a halt, which was
complied with. We now dismounted and the chief with much cere-

mony put tippets about our necks, such as they themselves wore.*
I readily perceived that this was to disguise us and owed its origin
to the same cause already mentioned. To give them further confidence, I put my cocked hat with feather on the chief and my
over shirt being of the Indian form, my hair dishevelled, and skin
well browned with the sun, I wanted no further addition to make
a complete Indian in appearance. The men followed my example,
and we were soon completely metamorphosed.

I again repeated to them the possibility of the party not having arrived at the place which I expected they were, but assured
them they could not be far below, lest by not finding them at the
forks their suspicions might arise to such height as to induce them
to return precipitately. We now set out and rode briskly within
sight of the forks, making one of the Indians carry the flag that
our own party should know who we were.

When we arrived in sight at the distance of about two miles
I discovered to my mortification that the party had not arrived and
the Indians slackened their pace. I now scarcely knew what to do
and feared every moment when they would halt altogether. I now
determined to restore their confidence, cost what it might, and
therefore gave the chief my gun and told him that if his enemies
were in those bushes before him that he could defend himself
with that gun, that for my own part I was not afraid to die, and if
I deceived him he might make what use of the gun he thought
proper, or in other words that he might shoot me. The men also
gave their guns to other Indians, which seemed to inspire them
with more confidence. They sent their spies before them at some
distance and when I drew near the place I thought of the notes
which I had left and directed Drouillard to go with an Indian man
and bring them to me, which he did; the Indian seeing him take
the notes from the stake on which they had been placed. I now

* The mantle was composed of 140 ermine skins. Lewis carried it back to
civilization where Charles Willson Peale used it to clothe a wax figure he had
made of the captain to display in his Philadelphia museum.

had recourse to a strategem in which I thought myself justified by the occasion, but I must confess set a little awkward. It had its desired effect. After reading the notes, which were the same I had left, I told the chief that when I had left my brother chief with the party where the river entered the mountain that we both agreed not to bring the canoes higher up than the next forks of the river above us, wherever this might happen; that there he was to wait my return, should he arrive first, and that in the event of his not being able to travel as fast as usual from the difficulty of the water, that he was to send up to the first forks above him and leave a note informing me where he was; that this note was left here today and that he informed me that he was just below the mountains and was coming on slowly up, and added that I should wait here for him. But if they did not believe me that I should send a man at any rate to the chief and they might also send one of their young men with him; that myself and two others would remain with them at this place. This plan was readily adopted and one of the young men offered his services. I promised him a knife and some beads as a reward for his confidence in us. Most of them seemed satisfied, but there were several that complained of the chief's exposing them to danger unnecessarily and said that we told different stories. In short, a few were much dissatisfied.

I wrote a note to Capt. Clark by the light of some willow brush and directed Drouillard to set out early, being confident that there was not a moment to spare. The chief and five or six others slept about my fire and the others hid themselves in various parts of the willow brush to avoid the enemy whom they were fearful would attack them in the course of the night. I now entertained various conjectures myself with respect to cause of Capt. Clark's detention and was even fearful that he had found the river so difficult that he had halted below the Rattlesnake Bluffs. I knew that if these people left me that they would immediately disperse and secrete themselves in the mountains where it would be impossible to find them, or at least in vain to pursue them, and that they would spread the alarm to all other bands within our reach and of course we should be disappointed in obtaining horses, which would vastly retard and increase the labor of our voyage, and I feared might so discourage the men as to defeat the expedition altogether. My mind was in reality quite as gloomy all this evening, as the most affrighted Indian, but I affected cheerfulness to keep the Indians so who were about me. We finally laid down and the chief placed himself by the side of my mosquito bier. I slept but little, as might well be expected, my mind dwelling on the state of the expedition which I have ever held in equal estimation with my own existence, and the fate of which appeared at this moment to depend in great measure upon the caprice of a few savages who are ever as fickle as the wind.

I had mentioned to the chief several times that we had with us a woman of his nation who had been taken prisoner by the Minitari, and that by means of her I hoped to explain myself more fully than I could do by signs. Some of the party had also told the Indians that we had a man with us who was black and had short, curling hair. This had excited their curiosity very much, and they seemed quite as anxious to see this monster as they were the merchandise which we had to barter for their horses.

Chapter 24

Horse Trading

After the expedition had been reunited, Sacagawea moved forward to interpret. "She came into the tent, sat down, and was beginning to interpret, when in the person of Cameahwait she recognized her brother. She instantly jumped up, and ran and embraced him, throwing over him her blanket and weeping profusely. The chief was himself moved, though not in the same degree. After some conversation between them, she resumed her seat and attempted to interpret for us, but her new situation seemed to overpower her, and she was frequently interrupted by her tears."

The council proceeded slowly for other reasons than Sacagawea's tears. The captains' words had to go to Labiche, who put them into French, to Charbonneau, who put them into Minitari, to Sacagawea, who put them into the Snake (or Sloshone) language. But they made the point that one of the purposes of the expedition was to find a way to bring trading goods, guns among them, to the Shoshones, and thus "it was mutually advantageous to them as well as to ourselves that they should render us such aids as they had it in their power to furnish in order to hasten our voyage and, of course, our return home." Cameahwait said he would do all he could to help. Medals and presents were then passed out—a red uniform coat, a shirt, a pair of scarlet leggings, a carrot of tobacco to Cameahwait; lesser presents to the lesser chiefs. Vermillion, moccasin awls, knives, beads, and looking glasses were distributed among the tribe along with some lyed corn, "which was the first they had ever eaten in their lives." Lewis shot off the air gun, which the astonished natives called "great medicine."

Everything about the expedition astonished the Indians—"the appearance of the men, their arms, the canoes, our manner of working them, the black man York, and the sagacity of my dog equally objects of admiration." They, unlike Indians previously met along the Missouri, were virtually untouched by civilization. They had no axes or hatchets, only a few knives—they used slivers of flint for cutting—and two or three ineffectual guns. They were desperately poor, often having no meat and forced to subsist on roots and berries. From May until early September they lived in the mountains hiding out from the Plains Indians who, armed with guns, raided them at will and stole their horses, the one thing they had in abundance. In the fall, joined by the Flatheads and other tribes of their own nation, they felt strong enough to migrate to the prairies to hunt buffalo. They were a likable people, gentle, courteous, "very orderly and do not crowd about our camp nor attempt to disturb any article they see lying about. They borrow knives, kettles, etc., from the men and always carefully return them." They knew nothing of whisky. They did know venereal disease, but this only convinced Lewis that since they had not previously met white men syphilis and gonorrhea "are native disorders of America." As with tribes along the Missouri, "the chastity of their women is not held in high estimation, . . . tho' they are not so importunate that we should caress their women as the Sioux were." The captains' sex lecture to the men did not attempt to prevent the "mutual exchange of good offices." They knew this was "impossible to effect, particularly on the part of our young men, whom some months of abstinence have made very polite to those tawny damsels." They only asked them to give the males "no cause of jealousy by having connection with their women without their knowledge."

After the Indian council the captains settled on a plan of action. Clark the next day would go ahead to study the Salmon River and determine whether the expedition should move ahead by land or water. To save time if he found the river navigable he would take with him eleven hunters and choppers to build dugouts. These would be ready to launch by the time Lewis and the rest of the party arrived with the baggage.

Clark's group left early August 18. Lewis directed the repacking of everything into parcels that could be carried on horseback. His years in the army made this "a business which I fortunately had not to learn on this occasion," though a shortage of materials for pack saddles forced him to improvise. "We find ourselves at a loss for nails and boards; for the first we substitute thongs of rawhide, which answer very well, and for the last had to cut off the blades of our oars and use the plank of some boxes which have heretofore held other articles, and put those articles into sacks of rawhide which I have had made for the purpose. By this means I have obtained as many boards as will make twenty saddles, which I suppose will be sufficient for our present exigencies."

He ended his journal entry for the day on a solemn note.

This day I completed my thirty-first year, and conceived that I had in all human probability now existed about half the period which I am to remain in this subluminary world. I reflected that I had as yet done but little, very little indeed, to further the happiness of the human race or to advance the information of the succeeding generation. I viewed with regret the many hours I have spent in indolence, and now solely feel the want of that information which those hours would have given me had they been judiciously expended. But since they are past and cannot be re-called, I dash[ed] from me the gloomy thought, and resolved in future to redouble my exertions and at least endeavor to promote those two primary objects of human existence, by giving them the aid of that portion of talents which nature and fortune have bestowed on me; or in future to live for mankind, as I have here-tofore lived for myself.

A week passed before the expedition moved out. The new cache took longer than usual because it had to be made surrepti-tiously at night three-quarters of a mile downstream from the Indians. It took a good part of a day to weight the canoes with stones and sink them in a nearby pond. Another day passed smok-ing and chatting while Cameahwait described in circumstantial detail the perils of the Salmon River. The chief heaped hills of sand on the ground to represent "the vast mountains of rock eternally covered with snow through which the river passed." The mountains were inaccessible, the river filled with roaring rapids that beat the water "into perfect foam as far as the eye could reach," and the banks hemmed by cliffs of rocks. He told of the Pierced Nose, or, Nez Perce, Indians who lived beyond the moun-tains on a river that "ran a great way toward the setting sun and finally lost itself in a great lake of water which was illy tasted and where the white men lived." Buffalo did not exist west of the mountains; the Nez Perce crossed the Rockies to hunt them in the plains. The road they took was "a very bad one" and they "suffered excessively with hunger on the route, being obliged to subsist for many days on berries alone, as there was no game in that part of the mountains, which were broken, rocky, and so thickly covered with timber that they could scarcely pass." Lewis was "perfectly satisfied that if the Indians could pass these mountains with their women and children, that we could also pass them."

Cameahwait convinced him the expedition must go overland to reach the Columbia. After the talk Lewis began to bargain in earnest for horses. At first, the Indians seemed willing to sell. He bought five "very reasonably, or at least for about the value of six dollars a piece in merchandise," and two days later three more for a handkerchief, some vermillion, and a battle axe Shields had hammered out back at Fort Mandan. He paid twice that for a mule but thought it "a great acquisition." At that point the Indians said they had nothing more for sale. When the Flatheads arrived from their home on the Bitterroot River, the tribe would need every horse in the village for the annual pilgrimage down to the plains. True, Cameahwait said, staring at Lewis, "his fierce eyes and lank jaws grown meager for the want of food," they would trade for guns. Lewis said he had none to spare. He tried to soften up the opposition through the stomach. He boiled up a meal of corn and beans for the whole tribe. He had the men make a brush drag and "in about two hours they caught 528 very good fish, most of them large trout," and most of which "I distributed . . . among the Indians." He gave Cameahwait some dried squashes brought from Fort Mandan. The chief "declared them to be the best thing he had ever tasted except sugar." (Sacagawea had given him a lump lifted from the expedition's larder.) He wished "his nation could live in a country where they could provide such food." Lewis said it would not be long before the white man would have it in his power to grant that wish. Still the Indians would sell no more horses. Lewis figured the party needed at least twenty-five for the trip through the mountains. He had only nine and a mule when the expedition left for the Indian village.

The Indians would not sell but they would loan their horses to get the Voyage of Discovery moving again, and on August 24 Lewis had "the inexpressible satisfaction to find myself once more underway with all my baggage and party." The caravan had made only six miles when an Indian rode up to say one of the men had fallen sick. The captain rode back to find Wiser "very ill with a fit of the colic." He prescribed a dose of the essence of peppermint and laudanum in a cup of water and this "in the course of half an hour so far recovered him that he was enabled to ride my horse and I proceeded on foot and rejoined the party."

The next morning, while Lewis rode along thinking of ways to entice a couple dozen more horses from the Indians, Charbonneau handed him a shock. Nonchalantly, he said Cameahwait had sent a messenger ahead to the Flatheads telling them to be ready tomorrow to move with the Snakes and all their horses down to the plains. This meant the expedition would be stranded without transportation. Charbonneau had known about this since early morning and said nothing. Lewis, enraged—or as he put it, "I could not forebear speaking to him with some degree of asperity on this occasion"—called a conference with Cameahwait and two lesser chiefs. Had they not promised to carry the baggage at least to Capt. Clark's camp on the Salmon River? Yes. They knew, did they not, that "if they wished the white men to be their friends and to assist them against their enemies by furnishing them with arms and keeping their enemies from attacking them that they must never promise us anything which they did not mean to perform?" Had not Capt. Lewis always and generously divided food from his stores and all that his hunters brought in with them? Cameahwait sat silently for some time, then said he had "done wrong," that the need of his people for food had driven him to act rashly, "but as he had promised to give me his assistance he would not in future be worse than his word."

The caravan moved on. The next day it paused "at the extreme source of the Missouri," where all the men "drank of the water and consoled themselves with the idea of having at length arrived at this long wished for point." During the afternoon one of the squaws leading two pack horses dropped behind, turning over the reins to a friend. "I inquired of Cameahwait the cause of her detention, and was informed by him in an unconcerned manner that she had halted to bring forth a child and would soon overtake us. In about an hour the woman arrived with her newborn babe and passed us on her way to the camp, apparently as well as she ever was."

At the edge of the Indian's village Cameahwait asked a favor.

Would the white men fire a volley from the rim overlooking it? Lewis "drew up the party at open order in a single rank and gave them a running fire, discharging two rounds." The Indians were "much gratified with this exhibition," and the procession moved on. Lewis was taken to a lodge erected in the center of the village especially for him. He raised a large flag alongside it and gave the chief one of equal size which to raise next to his lodge.

The party arrived at six in the evening. They found Colter there with a letter from Clark—all that Cameahwait had said about the Salmon was true: it was impassable. His guide, nicknamed "Old Toby," knew the Nez Perce road over the mountains and would lead the expedition along it. Clark "found it folly to think of attempting to descend this river in canoes," and urged Lewis to accept Old Toby's offer. Lewis repeated the contents of the letter to Cameahwait and then said he wanted to buy twenty horses. The chief gave his blessing and hoped "his people would spare me the number I wished."

Lewis, the diplomat, "determined to keep the Indians in a good humor, if possible, and to lose no time in obtaining the necessary number of horses." First, he told the hunters to be ready to beat the bushes next day for game to feed the Indians. Full stomachs should make bargaining easier. Next, he "directed the fiddle to be played, and the party danced very merrily, much to the amusement and gratification of the natives, though I must confess that the state of my own mind at this moment did not well accord with the prevailing mirth, as I somewhat feared that the caprice of the Indians might suddenly induce them to withhold their horses from us, without which my hopes of prosecuting my voyage to advantage was lost."

Chapter 25

Overland

By August 28 Lewis had wheedled twenty-two horses from the Indians, but each of the three he bought that day cost twice what he had previously paid, and the natives said there would be no more sales except in exchange for guns. When Clark rejoined the party he had to give up a knife and a pistol with powder and balls for one horse and a musket for another.

The expedition set out on August 30. Everyone expected a hard but not intolerable trip ahead. Old Toby told the men he would "show us a hilly, rough road over the mountains" which in ten days would take them to a navigable river. Fifteen days from that point they would be tasting salt water. The trek started well. The first full day on the road they made twenty miles, about what they had done during a good day on the water and with much less effort. Then, on September 1, the route edged into the mountains. Old Toby took them over one "nearly as steep as the roof of a house." Choppers had to move ahead to cut a path through fallen timber and thickets of pine trees. Several horses "fell over back-wards and rolled to the foot of the hills" and the men "were then obliged to carry the loads up the hills and then load again." Some-times they traveled along the bottoms of a river that twisted around the base of the mountains, but even that route offered little respite. The bottoms were "narrow and swampy" and made such "horrid, bad going" the men named one stretch Dismal Swamp. Then came more mountains, more work for the choppers, more tum-bling horses. Every day ended with "much fatigue and hunger." The hunters turned up little game. One night the temperature dropped sharply—no one knew how far because the last ther-mometer had just been broken—and the men awoke to find all the rawhide coverings frozen stiff. The party could not move out until they had been thawed flexible enough to cover the baggage.

They emerged from the mountains into the Bitterroot Valley on September 4 to be greeted by a village of some four hundred Flatheads. They were friendly but odd Indians—stouter, lighter complected than those met with previously and they spoke "the strangest language of any we have ever seen," uttering their words with a gurgling sound as if they had "an impediment in their speech or a brogue or burr on their tongue." Their light skin and peculiar language convinced the party it had come upon remnants of the mythical Welsh Indians.

They stayed three days with the Flatheads. The captains held the usual council, now more tedious than ever with one more link required in the chain of interpreters. The Indians gave no hint the party had an ordeal ahead. "They tell us that we can go in six days to where white traders come and that they had seen bearded men who came from a river to the north of us six days' march." The Flatheads had some five hundred "elegant" horses and though they were preparing to strike their village and join the Snakes for the trip to the plains they let the captains buy several and swap those that had gone lame in the mountains for healthy mounts.

The party moved out with forty good pack horses and three colts. They traveled down a valley flanked on the west by the soaring, saw-toothed Bitterroot range which must soon, somehow, be crossed. They made good time, nearly seventy miles in three days, and on September 9 reached a stream bearing west which the guide said they would follow into the mountains. The captains named it Traveler's Rest Creek after deciding to pause here to recoup the men and horses and let the hunters build up a stockpile of meat. The hunters found the area stripped of game.

On September 12, the first of a ten-day ordeal, Old Toby led the caravan along the ridge of a mountain that was "very painful to the horses, as we were obliged to go over steep stony sides of hills and along the hollows and ravines, rendered more disagreeable by the fallen timber. . . ." The hunters flushed only a pheasant for dinner. The next day, Friday the thirteenth, the guide got lost and took them several miles out of the way. The following evening, with the hunters still unsuccessful, Lewis brought out the portable soup he had purchased in Philadelphia. "Some of the men did not relish this soup" and voted to kill a colt for dinner, which was done. On the fourteenth Old Toby got lost again and carried the party down from the ridge they had been traveling into the gorge of the Lochsa River. They stumbled through it for a day before realizing the trail they should be on lay on the ridge. The trip back up was a nightmare. Several of the horses slipped and tumbled down the steep inclines. One carrying Clark's desk and trunk rolled over and over until a stout tree stopped its descent; the desk was shattered but the horse "escaped without much injury." Another time one of the horses rolled down a hillside "which was nearly perpendicular and strewed with large irregular rocks, nearly a hundred yards, and did not stop till he fell into the creek. We all expected he was killed, but to our astonishment on taking off his load he rose and seemed but little injured and in twenty minutes proceeded with his load."

The ridge once regained offered the party a dispiriting view of nothing but "high rugged mountains in every direction." Night caught them at a desolate spot without water. They dined on the remains of the killed colt and portable soup made from melted snow. The next day, September 16, opened on a bleaker note. The men awoke and to their "great surprise" found themselves and the ground covered with snow. Clark somehow at the end of the day had the energy to record what passed.

Began to snow about three hours before day and continued all day. The snow in the morning four inches deep on the old snow, and by night we found it from six to eight inches deep. I walked in front to keep the road and found great difficulty in keeping it as in many places the snow had entirely filled up the track and obliged me to hunt several minutes for the track. At twelve o'clock we halted on the top of the mountain to warm and dry ourselves a little as well as to let our horses rest and graze a little on some long grass which I observed. The knobs, steep hillsides, and falling timber continue today, and a thickly timbered country of eight different kinds of pine, which are so covered with snow that in passing thro' them we are continually covered with snow. I have been wet and as cold in every part as I ever was in my life. Indeed, I was at one time fearful my feet would freeze in the thin moccasins which I wore. After a short delay in the middle of the day, I took one man and proceeded on as fast as I could about six miles to a small branch passing to the right, halted and built fires for the party against their arrival, which was at dusk, very cold and much fatigued. We encamped at this branch in a thickly timbered bottom which was scarcely large enough for us to lie level. Men all wet, cold, and hungry. Killed a second colt which we all supped heartily on and thought it fine meat.

I saw four deer today and what is singular snapped seven times at a large buck. It is singular as my gun has a steel fusee and never snapped seven times before. In examining her found the flint loose. To describe the road of this day would be a repetition of yesterday except the snow which made it much worse.

Another cold, wet day followed. That night they killed the last colt and washed down the cuts with portable soup. The slim diet, "joined with fatigue, has a visible effect on our health. The men are growing weak and losing their flesh very fast; several are afflicted with dysentery and eruptions of the skins are very common." The next morning Clark took six hunters and moved out ahead of the main party to search for game. Twenty miles along the trail he saw "with inexpressible joy" through a break in the trees "an immense plain and level country" in the distance. With that vision in their heads the hunting party moved on and camped that night by a stream they called Hungry Creek. They had not eaten all day. The next morning they came upon a wild horse which they killed, ate part of, and hung the rest for the party coming up.

On September 20, Clark emerged from the mountains onto "a level pine country; proceeded on through a beautiful country for three miles to a small plain" and there found an Indian village. He lured two frightened youngsters with trinkets, and they led the way to the tribe's chief. The squaws served up a meal—some dried salmon, berries, a bread made of camas root—and soon after eating all were sick from having gorged on food their stomachs were not accustomed to. The next day the hunters fanned the area for game but found none. Clark bought a horse load of roots, berries, and salmon and sent it with Reuben Field and an Indian to meet Lewis' party. Food and the starving men came together eight miles from the Indian village. "I ordered the party to halt for the purpose of taking some refreshment," Lewis said. "I divided the fish, roots, and berries, and was happy to find a sufficiency to satisfy completely all our appetites."

The party reached the Indian village at five o'clock. It had taken them three and a half months to cross the mountains. "The pleasure I now felt in having triumphed over the Rocky Mountains," Lewis wrote in his journal, "and descending once more to a level and fertile country where there was every rational hope of finding a comfortable subsistence for myself and party can be more readily conceived than expressed, nor was the flattering prospect of the final success of the expedition less pleasing."

Part Four

Denouement

Chapter 26

Fort Clatsop

During the expedition, Lewis and Clark discovered 24 Indian tribes, 178 plants, and 122 animals then unknown to the world. All the tribes but one (the Blackfeet), two-thirds of the plants, and over half the animals were found west of the Rocky Mountains—but not on the outbound journey. Once through the mountains the rest of the westbound trip was an anti-climatic race to the ocean. The party left the Nez Perce villages and started down the Clearwater in five dugouts on October 7. They passed through some of the strangest, most awesome land yet encountered but paid it little attention in their eagerness to reach the coast. "Great joy in camp," Clark wrote in his journal exactly a month after leaving the Nez Perce. "We are in view of the ocean . . . this great Pacific Ocean." The miserable month that followed diluted that joy. "The sea," wrote Clark on December 1, "which is immediately in front, roars like a repeated rolling thunder and have roared in that way since our arrival in its borders, which is now

Clark's drawing of a Brant, discovered March 8, 1806

twenty-four days since we arrived in sight of the Great Western Ocean—I can't say Pacific as since I have seen it, it has been the reverse. Its waters are foaming and perpetually break with immense waves on the sands and rocky coasts, tempestuous and horrible." The sea roared through days filled with interminable rain interspersed with winds that often "blew with great violence." Everyone sloshed about in clothes "all rotten from being continually wet." The usually unemotional Clark was finally driven to remark: "O! how disagreeable is our situation during this dreadful weather."

After weeks of searching, the captains settled on a spot for their winter fort. It lay on the south side of the bay beyond the sound of the sea and close to an area where the neighboring Clatsop Indians said herds of elk, which would be the main source of food for the party, liked to graze. The men began building Fort Clatsop on December 7. On Christmas Day everyone was "snugly fixed" within, but otherwise the day offered little to cheer about. There was nothing "to raise our spirits"—that is, all had to solace "thirst

with our only beverage, pure water"—"or even gratify our appetites. Our dinner consisted of poor elk, so much spoiled that we
eat it through mere necessity, some spoiled pounded fish, and a
few roots." The day gave a dismal forecast of the winter ahead—
no whisky, no tobacco once the paltry supply on hand had been
chewed and smoked, a dull diet that ran mostly to boiled roots
and lean elk, damp rainy days without end—only twelve days all
winter were free of rain and six of those were overcast—that kept
the men close to the fort and soon made them victims of cabin
fever. Repeatedly, the journals acknowledged the relentless boredom with such entries as "nothing transpired" today, "no occurrences worthy of mention," "not anything transpired during the
day worthy of notice." Boredom as much as the abominable
weather led to an abnormal number of illnesses. "We have not
had as many sick at one time since we left Wood River," Lewis
said after the men had been cooped up in the fort for two months.
Most of the complaints stemmed from heavy colds accompanied
by "obstinate tho' not very high" fevers. But Dr. Lewis' practice
had variety. One day Ordway was "complaining of a cold and head-
ache"; another, Willard had badly split his knee with a tomahawk;
or Joseph Field "suffered from boils on his legs"; or Drouillard
came in with "a violent pain in his side." Gibson, out on a hunting
excursion, became so ill "that he could not set up or walk alone"
and had to be carried back to the fort. He arrived "a good deal
reduced and very languid"; the men had mentally placed him on
the death list, but Lewis thought he would live. He dosed him with
diluted nitre, "made him drink plentifully of sage tea," bathed his
feet in warm water, and at bedtime gave him thirty-five drops of
laudanum. Five days later Gibson was on "the recovery fast." Lewis'
rate of cures was close to perfect. Bratton was his only failure.
Early on Bratton had come down with a pain in his back; it per-
sisted all winter and with the arrival of spring he was "so much
reduced" that Lewis feared he might die.

Sick or well, the days passed and the men survived. The com-
pliant Indian women offered some consolation, but the men ap-

Salal, discovered January 20,
1806, hand-colored engraving
by W. Hooker
LIBRARY, THE ACADEMY OF
NATURAL SCIENCES OF
PHILADELPHIA

proached them gingerly after learning venereal disease, caught from the crews of American trading ships, was rampant among the coastal tribes. Among his patients Lewis listed only Goodrich and McNeal as victims of the pox.

The hunters were kept busy tracking the game through nearly impenetrable forests. A task force sent to the coast boiled thousands of gallons of sea water to produce twenty gallons of salt. The tailors made shirts and trousers and moccasins—338 pairs of moccasins by late March—from elk hides. Early in January Clark took a sightseeing party to the coast to gaze upon a whale that had been beached during a storm. Sacagawea, who had not yet seen the ocean, insisted she be taken along. She told Clark she "had traveled a long way with us to see the great waters, and that now that monstrous fish was also to be seen she thought it very hard that she could not

Oregon grape holly,
discovered April 11, 1806,
hand-colored engraving by
W. Hooker
LIBRARY, THE ACADEMY OF
NATURAL SCIENCES OF
PHILADELPHIA

be permitted to see either." Clark took her.

The trip for Clark was a holiday from the map he had been drawing "of the country through which we have passed from Fort Mandan to this place." When he showed the completed map to Lewis on February 11, it became clear at a glance what Old Toby had told them back at Traveler's Rest Creek—that they had gone, as Clark now figured it, some six hundred miles out of their way and wasted over a month and a half in unnecessary travel by following the Missouri to its headwaters. "We now discover that we have found the most practicable and navigable passage across the continent of North America," Clark boasted. Pleased as he was with the discovery, he knew it shattered a dream as old as America —that of an all-water route across the continent. Even the shortened route involved two considerable overland treks.

The captains had had no choice but to follow the Missouri on the way out because they were bound by the President's instructions to do so and because they knew that at its headwaters were the Snake (or Shonshoni) Indians who had the horses that would carry them and their provisions over the Rocky Mountains. But on the homebound trip they were free to test the new route. Instead of traveling down one side and up the other of a trail that resembled the sides of an equilateral triangle, they would move in an easterly direction across the base of the triangle from Traveler's Rest Creek to Medicine River, which joined the Missouri just above the Great Falls. A trip that took fifty-three days coming out they expected to do in four going back.

Except for the remarks on the revelations emitted by his map, Clark had little to say to posterity about the soggy stay at Fort Clatsop. On 1 January 1806 he ceased to keep his journal. Lewis on that day, after a lapse of several months, began his again, and Clark copied almost verbatim his own entries from Lewis'. Occasionally he would alter a word. When Lewis said that the sea otter's "is the richest and I think most delicious fur in the world," Clark altered "delicious" to "delightful."

Lewis used his journal to fight boredom. The early entries were short warm-up exercises sometimes laced with the remark that "nothing interesting occurred today," but at the end of the first week he slipped in a long, vivid paragraph about the Indians in the neighborhood.

The Clatsops, Chinooks, and Killamucks, etc., are very loquacious and inquisitive. They possess good memories and have repeated to us the names, capacities of the vessels, etc., of many traders and others who have visited the mouth of this river. They are generally low in stature, proportionally small, rather lighter complected, and much more ill-formed than the Indians of the Missouri and those of our frontier. They are generally cheerful but never gay. With us their conversation generally turns upon the subjects of trade, smoking, eating, or their women; about the latter they speak without

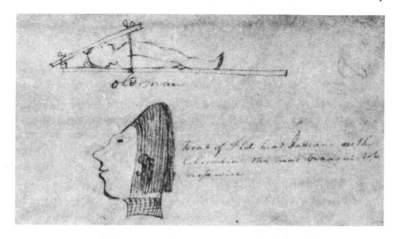

Clatsop Indians, drawing by Clark

reserve in their presence of their every part and of the most familiar connection. They do not hold the virture of their women in high estimation, and will even prostitute their wives and daughters for a fishing hook or a strand of beads. In common with other savage nations they make their women perform every species of domestic drudgery, but in almost every species of this drudgery the men also participate. Their women are also compelled to gather roots and assist them in taking fish, which articles form much the greatest part of their subsistence. Notwithstanding the servile manner in which they treat their women they pay much more respect to their judgment and opinions in many respects than most Indian nations. Their women are permitted to speak freely before them, and sometimes appear to command with a tone of authority. They generally consult them in their traffic and act in conformity to their opinions.

In the days that followed, Lewis described the Indians' elegant canoes, their houses, their handsome baskets and conical hats woven from reeds, how they treated venereal disease, their food, and how they cooked it. If the passages had been sorted out from

the daily entries, pieced together into a running essay, and published during his lifetime, Lewis would have been known as a
distinguished ethnologist.

The same could be said about his entries on the flora and
fauna of the neighborhood, about which he also wrote at length
during the incarceration at Fort Clatsop. He had a plan in mind.
Toward the end of January he began to intersperse in the entries
comments on plants indigenous to the region—a unique thistle, a
peculiar fern—and from then until mid-February he described the
flora, beginning with fruit and berry bushes, moving on to shrubs,
then finally to trees. Although the trees had lost their leaves and
the flowers had shriveled under winter skies Lewis still managed to
turn up ten new plants, nine of which he somehow in that damp
climate dried sufficiently in the plant press to preserve for posterity.

On February 15, Lewis abruptly abandoned botany and announced in the journal he would now write on the "quadrupeds
of this country from the Rocky Mountains to the Pacific Ocean."
Again he approached his subject systematically but not enslaved
to a rigid outline. One day a member of the crew would bring in
what looked like a new species of buzzard, and the next day another would bring Lewis "a specimen of pine peculiar to the
swamps." Each time Lewis interrupts his discussion of quadrupeds

Head of a vulture, drawing by Clark

to describe what the men have turned up, then that done, goes back to his animals—the red deer, mule deer, elk, tiger cat (bobcat), silver fox, antelope, sheep (that is, mountain goat, which Indians described but no one in the expedition ever saw), and sea otter. He pauses for a long entry on the delicious eulachlon which had begun to run and which the Indians had taught the crew how to catch and to cook, then again returns to the animals— the raccoon, various squirrels, badger, rat, panther, hare, polecat, and skunk. Here, in a shift in the plan, he mixes in descriptions of animals found only east of the mountains.

On March 1, still very much organized, Lewis moves into birds. First come the terrestrial birds—the prairie hen, cock of the plains (sage grouse), pheasant, raven, turtle dove, robin, lark, vulture, snipe, lark, curler—then five days later he turns to acquatic birds—herons, cranes, four species of gulls, loons, grebes, geese, swans, ducks. On March 11, about the time that final preparations for the homebound trek are underway, Lewis' neat plan falls apart. He jumps about from a description in one entry of snakes and snails to the eagle, then to fish—porpoise, skate, flounder, salmon—then back to birds, then on to clams. The disarray of these final entries did not detract from Lewis' impressive achievements as a zoologist. In less than a month he had written sometimes lengthy, always accurate, descriptions of more than a hundred animals native to the lower Columbia and in the process turned up twenty-three species or sub-species then unknown to science.

The journal was the staff that carried Lewis through a dull winter, but by mid-March he had clearly tired of it. Signs of spring were in the air—the elk were shedding their horns, the birds had begun again to sing—and he, like the men, wanted to start moving upstream. All knew that ahead lay the hardest stretch of the long trip. They must trek again through the arid region that flanked the upper Columbia where there was little game, then back into the mountains which they knew were still clogged with snow. None of the men were fresh, several were sick, and several more weak. The hunters had been unable to accumulate a backlog

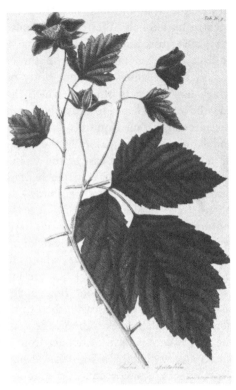

*Salmonberry, discovered
March 27, 1806, hand-
colored engraving by
W. Hooker*
LIBRARY, THE ACADEMY OF
NATURAL SCIENCES OF
PHILADELPHIA

of meat for the trip, and the salmon were at least a month away
from running. American trading ships were sure to arrive soon and
would be able to restock the expedition's nearly exhausted supply
of Indian presents and almost empty larder. But the mood of the
men was low—if they had sung or danced away a single evening

Large-headed clover, discovered
April 17, 1806, hand-colored
engraving by W. Hooker

since arriving at Fort Clatsop, the journals make no mention of it—and itchy feet infected the entire party. On Sunday, March 23, Lewis and Clark made perhaps their first serious misjudgment of the entire trip when "at 1 P.M. we bid a final adieu to Fort Clatsop."

Chapter 27

Once Again Those Tremendous Mountains

On April 19, the party completed ten days of portaging around a spot some twenty miles long where the Columbia cut through a range of mountains and dropped precipitously as it raced through rock-walled chutes. Above this wretched stretch of rapids and falls the men repeated in reverse a startlingly swift transition—from the lush, humid climate they had spent four dreary months in to a dry, semi-arid one blessed with a clear sky. Ahead lay a treeless plain that stretched for three hundred and fifty miles toward the Rocky Mountains and upon which, as the party had found on the way out, "there are no deer, antelopes, or elk on which we could depend for subsistence on any terms." The expedition would have to cross this plain on meager rations, for the Indians on the western edge could spare no provisions. They were waiting for the salmon run to begin. They could spare horses, but at outrageous prices that the expedition, now nearly stripped of its once large supply of Indian presents, could hardly afford. The Indians coveted the party's copper cooking kettles, and for several of these traded ten horses, somewhat fewer than needed to carry the party across the plains.

It was at this point that Lewis lost his temper. "I directed the horses to be hobbled and suffered to graze at a little distance from our camp under the immediate eye of the men who had them in charge. One of the men, Willard, was negligent in his attention to his horse and suffered it to ramble off. It was not to be found. . . . This, in addition to the other difficulties under which I labored, was truly provoking. I reprimanded him more severely for this piece of negligence than had been usual with me."

Given what had gone before and what Lewis knew lay ahead—his journals make clear that the forthcoming trek over "those tremendous mountains" haunted him—the outburst can be excused. But further incidents indicate he was no longer himself. Two days later Lewis caught an Indian stealing an iron socket off a canoe pole. He "gave him several severe blows and made the men kick him out of camp." The men were astonished, for as Gass remarked in his journal, this striking of an Indian by any man in the party "was the first act of the kind that had happened during the expedition." But Lewis had not finished. Having hit the Indian, he then told those who had seen the act that "the next man who attempted to steal should be shot . . . and [he] informed them that he would kill them in a moment and set their town on fire."

Two weeks later Lewis exploded again. The tribes along the Columbia had been both amused and astonished to learn that the white men would dine on dogs. The Indians had many dogs but never ate them. They gladly sold them to the expedition. One day, while Lewis was eating "an Indian fellow very impertinently threw a poor half-starved puppy nearly into my plate by way of derision for our eating dogs and laughed very heartily at his own impertinence." The act enraged—or as he put it, "provoked"—Lewis. "I was so provoked at his insolence that I caught the puppy and threw it with great violence at him and struck him in the breast and face, seized my tomahawk and showed him by signs if he repeated his insolence I would tomahawk him. The fellow withdrew apparently much mortified, and I continued my repast on *dog* without further molestation."

The tension exuded by Lewis—nothing in the journals even hints that Clark swung from his usual even-tempered self—soon spread to the men. The day after the puppy episode Drouillard and Colter, two of the steadiest members of the party, quarrelled. Two days later Lewis remarks that several of the hunters, who had been ordered to start searching for game at dawn, had remained in camp "without our permission or knowledge until late in the morning; we chid them severely for their indolence and inattention to the order last evening." (Clark's entry for the day says only, "this morning our hunters were out by the time it was light.")

By now the expedition had crossed the plains and was back among the Nez Perce. No one had had a clear view of the mountains yet, then on May 7 the clouds lifted. "The spurs of the Rocky Mountains, which were in view from the high plain today," Lewis wrote, "were perfectly covered with snow." On the heels of that awful sight the Indians gave worse news. "The Indians inform us that the snow is yet so deep on the mountains that we shall not be able to pass them until the next full moon or about the first of June; others set the time at still a more distant period. This is unwelcome intelligence to men confined to a diet of horsebeef and roots, and who are as anxious as we are to return to the fat plains of the Missouri and thence to our native homes."

The captains got this bad news on May 7. For the next month the party camped against the awesome backdrop of snow-capped mountains, a constant haunting spectacle, in no way beautiful to the men. "Even now," said Clark, speaking for all, "I shudder with the expectation of great difficulties in passing those mountains." By the first of June they had exhausted their paltry stock of trading goods—a few awls, some knitting needles, colored thread and

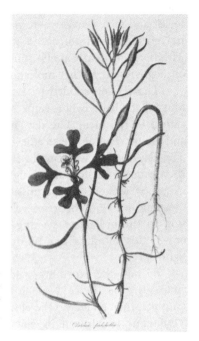

Ragged robin, or beautiful Clarkia, discovered June 1, 1806, hand-colored engraving by W. Hooker
LIBRARY, THE ACADEMY OF NATURAL
SCIENCES OF PHILADELPHIA

ribbons—and could no longer barter for provisions "to meet that wretched portion of our journey, the Rocky Mountains, where hunger and cold in their most rigorous forms assail the wearied traveler; not any of us have yet forgotten our suffering in those mountains in September last, and I think it probable we never shall."

Finally, they could stand waiting no longer. "Everybody seems anxious to be in motion, convinced that we have not now any time to delay if the calculation is to reach the United States this season." They set out on June 15 through a sheet of rain. No Indian had offered to guide them. They must depend on blaze marks made by Indians or the party on the way out to show them the way.

The lateness of spring in the foothills made everyone im-

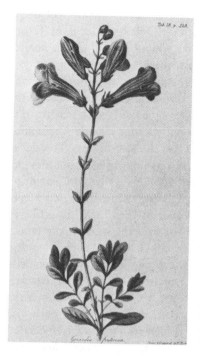

Shrubby penstemon, discovered in June 1806, hand-colored engraving by W. Hooker
LIBRARY, THE ACADEMY OF NATURAL SCIENCES OF PHILADELPHIA

mediately apprehensive. "These appearances in this comparatively low region augurs but unfavorably with respect to the practicability of passing the mountains. However, we determine to proceed." They changed their minds two days later when Clark, out in front searching for the trail, reached the top of a mountain. He found the packed snow there nearly fifteen feet deep.

Here was winter with all its rigors; the air was cold, my hands and feet were benumbed. We knew that it would require four days to reach the fish wier at the entrance of Colt Creek, provided we were so fortunate as to be enabled to follow the proper ridge of the mountains to lead us to that place. Of this all our most expert woodsmen and principal guides were extremely doubtful. Short of that point we could not hope for any food for our horses, not even under wood itself as the whole was covered many feet deep in snow. If we proceeded and should get bewildered in those mountains the certainty was that we should lose all of our horses and consequently our baggage, instruments, perhaps our papers, and thus eventually risk the loss of our discoveries which we had already made if we should be so fortunate as to escape with life. . . . Under these circumstances we conceived it madness in this stage of the expedition to proceed without a guide who could certainly conduct us to the fish wiers on the Kooskooske [Traveler's Rest Creek], as our horses could not possibly sustain a journey of more than four or five days without food. We therefore come to the resolution to return with our horses while they were yet strong and in good order, and endeavor to keep them so until we could procure an Indian to conduct us over the snowy mountains, and again to proceed as soon as we could procure such a guide, knowing from the appearance of the snows that if we remained until it had dissolved sufficiently for us to follow the road that we should not be enabled to return to the United States within this season. Having come to this resolution, we ordered the party to make a deposit of all the baggage which we had not immediate use for, and also all the roots and bread . . . which they had except an allowance for a few days to enable them to return to some place at which we could subsist by hunting until we procured a guide. We left our instruments, and I even left the most of my papers, believing them safer here than to risk them on horseback over the road, rocks, and water which we had passed. Our baggage being laid on scaffolds and well covered, we began our retrograde march at 1 P.M., having remained about three hours on this snowy mountain. We returned by the route we had advanced to Hungry Creek, which we ascended about two miles and encamped. We had here more grass for our horses than the preceding evening, yet it was but scant. The party were a good deal dejected, tho' not as much so as I had apprehended they would have been. This is the first time since we have been on this tour that we have ever been *compelled to retreat or make a retrograde march. It rained on us most of this evening.*

From the camp on Hungry Creek, the captains sent Drouillard and Shannon back to the Nez Perce to negotiate for guides. They could offer for pay up to three rifles with ammunition. While they were gone the party had to endure another retreat. The hunters could find no game in the vicinity of the aptly named Hungry Creek. And so backward through a "tedious and difficult part of our route, obstructed with brush and innumerable logs of fallen timber, which renders the traveling distressing and even dangerous to our horses," the men went glumly the next day. "We all felt some mortification in being thus compelled to retrace our steps."

Drouillard and Shannon returned on June 23 with three Indians "who had consented to accompany us to the falls of the Missouri for the compensation of two guns." The party set out the next morning, everyone in a relaxed mood when it became clear that the guides were "most admirable pilots." Once back in the high part of the mountains, where the snow was still deep, the traveling went easily. "The snow bore our horses very well and the traveling was infinitely better than the obstruction of rocks and fallen timber" met on the way out. Each day the caravan made twice the distance it had on the westbound trek.

Midway in the third day, while crossing a high ridge that offered a "scene sufficient to have dampened the spirits of any except such hardy travelers as we have become," the guides requested a halt to smoke a pipe. The party was now deep within the maze of massive pinnacles that stretched away on all sides as far as the eye could see. "From this place we had an extensive view of these stupendous mountains, principally covered with snow like that on which we stood. We were entirely surrounded by those mountains from which to one unacquainted with them it would have seemed impossible ever to have escaped. In short, without the assistance of our guides I doubt much whether we who

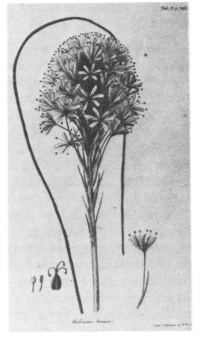

Beargrass: "The leaves are made use of by the natives to make baskets and other ornaments. On high land, Rocky Mountains, June 15, 1806," hand-colored engraving by W. Hooker
LIBRARY, THE ACADEMY OF
NATURAL SCIENCES OF
PHILADELPHIA

had once passed them could find our way to Traveler's Rest in their present situation, for the marked trees on which we had placed considerable reliance are much fewer and more difficult to find than we had apprehended." On June 29 they edged past the worst of the mountains and "bid adieu to the snow." The day after they descended to a plain, "leaving these tremendous mountains behind us, in passing of which we have experienced cold and hunger of which I shall ever remember," said Clark. Clark figured the party had traveled one hundred and forty miles through the mountains, "which for sixty miles are covered with eternal snows." But their road, hard as it was, was also clearly "the most practicable route which does exist across the continent by way of the Missouri and Columbia Rivers." The Indian guides said they would use it to return home, "a circumstance," said the captains, which "fur-

Western spring beauty, discovered
June 27, 1806, hand-colored
engraving by W. Hooker
LIBRARY, THE ACADEMY OF NATURAL
SCIENCES OF PHILADELPHIA

nishes sufficient evidence that there is not so near or so good a route to the plains of the Columbia by land along the river as that which we came." The dream of an all-water route had ended forever.

Chapter 28

"That Esteemable Man"

Back at Fort Clatsop the captains had agreed that at Traveler's Rest Creek the party would divide. Lewis with a group of volunteers would explore the overland shortcut to the Great Falls. His detachment would split there, leaving one contingent to prepare for the portage around the falls while the other went with Lewis to explore the Marias River to its source, which would mark the northward extent of the Louisiana Territory. Meanwhile, Clark with the remainder of the crew would return to the head of the Jefferson River and retrieve the boats left there. He, too, would divide his party, one group going downriver to join those at the head of the falls and help carry out the portage while Clark's traveled overland to explore the Yellowstone River down to where it met the Missouri and where everyone would rendezvous for the homeward stretch.

The two side excursions were being made to satisfy one of the President's instructions. He had said that to determine the boundaries with Canada and Spanish lands to the south "it becomes interesting to fix with precision" the source of the rivers that run into the Missouri. Clark's assignment was the easier. He would have with him Sacagawea, who knew the country, and the Indians they might meet were expected to be friendly. Lewis, however, would be traveling through territory roamed by the Blackfeet Indians, "a vicious, lawless, and rather an abandoned set of wretches." The expedition set off on its separate ways on July 3 with Clark full of foreboding. "I could not avoid feeling much concern on this occasion, although I hoped this separation was only momentary." It was. The splintered groups rejoined on August 12.

Except for the loss of all the horses to thieving Indians, plus the usual round of narrow escapes and hardships, Clark's excursion had gone well. Lewis' had not. His party reached the head of the falls of the Missouri with little trouble but found the cache left there last year had been flooded. All of Lewis' plant specimens collected from Fort Mandan on had been ruined. Miraculously, Clark's map of the river had survived. Lewis left the bulk of his party to retrieve the boats stashed below the falls. They would ride them down to the mouth of the Marias and wait there while Lewis, with Drouillard and the Field brothers explored the upper reaches of that river. A further disappointment followed. The Marias turned out to curve westward rather than north. After losing "all hope of the waters of this river ever extending to north latitude 50°," Lewis headed downstream. On the way his small group came upon eight Blackfeet. Lewis invited them to camp with him overnight. Early the next morning the Indians "treacherously seized on and made themselves master of all our guns—in which situation we engaged them with our knives and our pistols, recovered our guns, and killed two of them and put the others to flight, pursued them, retook our horses, excepting two which they had attempted to carry off and took from them fifteen horses, a gun, and several bows and quivers of arrows, shields, and all their baggage." During the next twenty-four hours he and the men rode, so he estimated, 142 miles over a terrain streaked with gulches barely perceivable as they pushed on through the night. By great luck they reached the Missouri just as the crew in the retrieved boats floated into view. "We now continued our route down the Missouri without interruption or material accident until the 11th August, when going in there with one of my hunters to kill some elk he mistook me from the color of my dress, which was leather from an elk, fired on me and hit me through the upper part of my thigh." Lewis passed over the incident lightly in his report of it to the President. "Fortunately, the ball missed the bone and being in good state of health I recovered rapidly," he said, adding that nothing further worth relating occurred until six weeks later when the Voyage of Discovery reached Saint Louis, ending its two-and-a-half-year trip to the Pacific Coast and back.

Lewis had begun his report to Jefferson while the boats were still gliding down the last stretch of the Missouri. Upon arriving at Saint Louis at noon on 23 September 1806, he recopied the rough draft and posted it off to Washington that day. In it he made two points emphatically. The first was that the captains were certain they had "discovered the most practicable route which does exist across the continent by means of the navigable branches of the Missouri and Columbia Rivers," that the route entailed 340 miles by land, 140 of them over "tremendous mountains which for 60 miles are covered with eternal snows," and that "we view this passage across the continent as affording immense advantages to the fur trade, but fear that the advantages which it offers as a communication for the productions of the East Indies to the United States and thence to Europe will never be found equal on an extensive scale to that by way of Cape of Good Hope." (Jefferson reacted curiously to this news. In some way he convinced himself it must be kept secret from the world. In the first draft of his message to Congress announcing Lewis and Clark's successful return he did mention they had "traversed the high mountains" separating the Missouri from the Columbia, but in the final version he said only, "they have traced the Missouri nearly to its source, descended the Columbia to the Pacific Ocean.")

Lewis made his second point near the end of the report: "With respect to the exertions and services rendered by that esteemable man Capt. William Clark in the course of the late voyage, I cannot say too much. If, sir, any credit be due for the success of that arduous enterprise in which we have been mutually engaged, he is equally with myself entitled to your consideration and that of our common country." Pointedly, as in all his letters to Jefferson, he referred to Clark as "captain." But now by implication he was also saying that the "arduous enterprise" should be known as the Lewis and Clark Expedition—and so he ever after called it. It was a request that must have startled Jefferson. Lewis had always called it "my expedition," had always said "I plan to do this," "I want this done." Now it was always "we view," "we believe," "we have discovered."

It became "our enterprise" sometime after the shakedown when they began referring regularly in the journals to "my friend Capt. Lewis" and "my friend Capt. Clark." By then the trust between them was complete and remained so to the end. Once, on the return trip, Clark set out to explore a tributary of the Columbia. While starting out he looked back to see four canoes of Indians "bending their course towards our camp, which at this time is very weak, Capt. Lewis having only ten men with him. I hesitated for a moment whether it would not be adviseable for me to return and delay until a part of our hunters should return to add more strength to our camp. But on a second reflection and reverting to the precautions always taken by my friend Capt. Lewis on those occasions banished all apprehensions and I proceeded on down."

But there are hints in the journals that the easy-going, imperturable Clark sometimes worried about his friend. Lewis could be moody, temperamental, and subject to depressions that came close to immobilizing him. The entire crew must have felt uneasy to see him for several days sitting aboard the barge when they traveled through country filled with plants and animals no one had ever seen before. He constantly had to check the rash streak in his

A Blackfoot Indian on Horseback, aquatint of watercolor
by Karl Bodmer

nature. The day Charbonneau for the second time nearly sank the white pirogue Lewis, watching from shore and knowing no man could swim the torrent of waves the wind was kicking up, "involuntarily dropped my gun, threw aside my shot pouch, and was in the act of unbuttoning my coat before I recollected the folly of the attempt I was about to make, which was to throw myself into the river and endeavor to swim to the pirogue." He could be sticky company. A Scotsman who visited the party at Fort Mandan said Lewis "could not make himself agreeable to us. He could speak fluently and learnedly on all subjects, but his inveterate disposition against the British stained, at least in our eyes, all his eloquence." Of Clark he said: "equally well informed, but his conversation was always pleasant, for he seemed to dislike giving offense unnecessarily."

Escape from Blackfeet, watercolor by Alfred Jacob Miller
WALTERS ART GALLERY, BALTIMORE

Given the enduring tradition that Clark fathered numerous children among tribes met on the trip, there is no reason to imagine sexual overtones in the close bond between them, yet the relationship did resemble that of a successful marriage where the partners accommodated themselves without attempting to change one another. Each had his favorites among the crew. Clark especially liked young Shannon, whom he invited after the expedition to join him as partner in a fur trading operation. He liked, too, the Charbonneau family—Sacagawea, whom he nicknamed "Janey"; her son Baptiste, whom he called "Pomp," and after whom he named a huge pile of rock found along the Yellowstone "Pompey's Rock"; and even the bumptious Charbonneau himself, in whom Lewis found "no peculiar merit" but to whom Clark said that "if you wish to live with white people, and will come to me, I will give you a piece of land and furnish you with horses, cows, and hogs." Lewis, on the other hand, favored the Field brothers, Shields, and, above all, Drouillard. Clark may have had mixed feelings about Drouillard. During the aborted first attempt to recross the Rockies, Lewis said "Drouillard, our principal dependence as a woodsman and guide," doubted the party could make it without Indian guides. Clark's otherwise identical entry in the journal alters that praise to read: "all of our most expert woodsmen and principal guides were extremely doubtful."

No hint of jealousy marred the friendship. On the slow haul up to the Mandan villages Clark ran the barge, charted the course of the river, kept the daily journal, yet not once, even in the more forthright rough draft of the journal, did he complain of carrying more than his share of the burden. Clark deferred to Lewis' superior education and let him draft all his correspondence likely to appear in the press. Lewis, in turn, acknowledged the fact Clark was superior as a riverman and scout and that he got along better with Indians. Lewis was the company physician from the start, but when Clark became a favorite with the Nez Perce, among whom he administered to forty or fifty patients a day during the protracted stay on the return trip, Lewis abdicated his position gracefully.

Surely Lewis told Clark of his determination to have their voyage known as the Lewis and Clark Expedition, and surely, though he demurred, Clark knew his sometimes headstrong friend would have his way. But Clark's sense of what was right probably shaped his decision to let Lewis have to himself whatever glory awaited in Washington. The captains left Saint Louis early in October, each headed for his own home. Lewis reached Washington on December 28, where a banquet had been arranged to honor the homecoming heroes. After waiting over two weeks for Clark's arrival, they held the banquet on 14 January 1807 without him.

Congress meanwhile had been wondering how the nation should reward all those who had shared in the Voyage of Discovery. In a letter to the chairman of the House committee appointed to deal with the problem, Secretary of War Dearborn recommended that every member be given double pay for his time of service and that each of the crew receive 320 acres of government land, that Clark receive 1,000 acres and Lewis 1,500 acres. He noted that Captain Lewis had emphatically urged that Corporal Warfington, who had brought the barge from the Mandan villages back to Saint Louis, and Private Newman, who had been discharged for insubordination, share in these rewards. He ended his letter saying: "It may be proper for me to remark that in a conversation with Captain Lewis, he observed that whatever grant of land Congress might think proper to make to himself and Lieutenant Clark, it was his wish there should be no distinction of rank so noticed as to make a difference in the quantity granted to each; and that he would prefer an equal division of whatever quantity might be granted to them."

On 3 March 1807 Congress, after some fuss, authorized the President to reward the crew, including Warfington and Newman, 320 acres each and double pay for the time they served. It granted the same double pay to the captains and authorized that both men be given 1,600 acres each of government land—all this, said in a bill that ended with words that could only have pleased Lewis, for the "late enterprise to the Pacific Ocean conducted by Messrs. Lewis and Clark."

Criminal + lesser got paid same as everyone - York got nothing

Chapter 29

"I Fear
O! I Fear"

On 11 October 1809, Meriwether Lewis, then governor of the Louisiana Territory, killed himself. Gilbert C. Russell, the commanding officer at Fort Pickering at Chickasaw Bluffs, Tennessee, described the events leading up to the tragedy in a letter to Jefferson.

Governor Lewis left Saint Louis late in August or early in September 1809 intending to go by the route of the Mississippi and the ocean to the city of Washington, taking with him all the papers relative to his expedition to the Pacific Ocean, for the purpose of preparing and putting them to the press, and to have some drafts paid which had been drawn by him on the government and protested. On the morning of the 15th of September, the boat in which he was a passenger landed him at Fort Pickering in a state of mental derangement, which appeared to have been produced as much by indisposition [intemperance] as other causes. The subscriber, being then the commanding officer of the fort, on discovering his situation, and learning from the crew that he had made two attempts to kill himself, in one of which he had nearly succeeded, resolved at once to take possession of him and his papers and detain them there until he recovered, or some friend might arrive in whose hands he could depart in safety.

In this condition he continued without any material change for about five days, during which time the most proper and efficacious means that could be devised to restore him was administered, and on the sixth or seventh day all symptoms of derangement disappeared and he was completely in his senses and thus continued for ten or twelve days. On the twenty-ninth of the same month he left Bluffs with the Chickasaw agent, the interpreter, and some of the chiefs, intending then to proceed the usual route thro' the Indian country, Tennessee, and Virginia to his place of destination, with his papers well secured and packed on horses. By much severe depletion [blood-letting] during his illness he had been considerably reduced and debilitated, from which he had not entirely recovered when he set off, and the weather in that country being yet excessively hot and the exercise of traveling too severe for him, in three or four days he was again affected with the same mental disease. He had no person with him who could manage or control him in his propensities, and he daily grew worse until he arrived at the house of a Mr. Grinder within the jurisdiction of Tennessee and only seventy miles from Nashville, where in the apprehension of being destroyed by enemies which had no existence but in his wild imagination, he destroyed himself in the most cool, desperate, and barbarian-like manner, having been left in the house entirely to himself. The night preceding this one of his horses and one of the Chickasaw agent's with whom he was traveling strayed off from the camp and in the morning could not be found. The agent, with some Indians, stayed to search for the horses, and Governor Lewis with their two servants and the baggage horses proceeded to Mr. Grinder's where he was to halt until the agent got up.

After he arrived there and refreshed himself with a little meal and drink he went to bed in a cabin by himself and ordered the servants to go to the stables and take care of the horses, least they might lose some that night. Some time in the night he got his pistols, which he loaded after everybody had retired in a separate building and discharged one against his forehead without much effect—the ball not penetrating the skull but only making a furrow over it. He then discharged the other against his breast where the ball entered and passing downward thro' his body came out low down near his backbone. After some time he got up and went to the house where Mrs. Grinder and her children were lying and asked for water, but her husband being absent and having heard the report of the pistols she was greatly alarmed and made him no answer. He then in returning got his razors from a portfolio which happened to contain them and sitting up in his bed was found about daylight by one of the servants busily engaged in cutting himself from head to foot. He again begged for water, which was given him, and so soon as he drank he lay down and died with the declaration to the boy that he had killed himself to deprive his enemies of the pleasure and honor of doing it. His death was greatly lamented. And that a fame so dearly earned as his should finally be clouded by such an act of desperation was to his friends still greater cause of regret.

The way Lewis died surprised neither Jefferson or Clark. "He was much afflicted and habitually so with hypochondria," Jefferson said, then alluding to the intemperance said to have dominated Lewis' last months added: "This was probably increased by the habit into which he had fallen and the painful reflections that would necessarily produce in a mind like his."

Clark heard the news of Lewis' death two weeks after it occurred. "I fear O! I fear the weight of his mind has overcome him," he said.

Epilogue:
The Eminent Dr. Barton

Jefferson considered Dr. Benjamin Smith Barton the ablest naturalist in America, but Lewis suspected soon after his return to civilization that the eminent Dr. Barton was something of a fraud. A year after the captain's death Barton confessed to Jefferson that "during the governor's last visit to Philadelphia there was some difference between him and me." Barton said the estrangement originated "*wholly* in the illiberal . . . conduct of some of my enemies here, who labored, not without some effect, to excite uneasiness in his mind, as to my friendship for him." Jefferson had asked Barton to edit for publication the scientific portions of Lewis' journals. The doctor agreed to do so and promised he would be "careful of his fame," meaning Lewis' but probably also his own. Jefferson replied at once that "with respect to his just reputation I know it will be safe in your hands." He could not have been more wrong. Nearly a century would pass before the world had more than a hint of the formidable scientific achievements of the Lewis and Clark expedition. Much that the expedition discovered that was then unknown to science had to be rediscovered through the nineteenth century, thanks largely to the eminent but derelict Dr. Barton.

Barton's credentials, so far as Jefferson knew, were impeccable. He had graduated from the University of Pennsylvania's medical school in 1786, gone on to further study at the University of Edinburgh, then on to London to work with Dr. John Coakley Lettsom and the renowned surgeon John Hunter. Jefferson met him in Paris in the summer of 1788. He gave a "vivid and favorable" first impression. He was a tall man with a strong face and "eyes inordinately large, black, and full of fire; and, by his affability and fluency in conversation, he exhibited those traits to great advantage." The following year he returned to Philadelphia to fill the vacant chair of botany at the university. Even his enemies admitted he was a superb teacher. "There can be no doubt that he did more than any of his contemporaries in diffusing a taste for the natural sciences among the young men who then resorted to that school." Botany up to then had in America been a field largely preempted by gifted amateurs like John and William Bartram. Barton made it academically respectable. No one in the country was better read than he in the scientific literature of the day.

Barton pioneered what in time would become a flourishing specialty in America—the academic charlatan. Although trained as a physician he specialized in natural history because, it would seem, this was the coming thing. "*Natural history* and *botany*," he wrote from England, "are the fashionable and favorite studies of the polite as well as the learned part of Europe. Whatever regards the *natural history* of America is particularly sought after." He tried while scampering up the ladder toward fame to latch on to the coattails of those ahead of him. An alert name-dropper, he reminded the world regularly of his friendship with Sir Joseph Banks, president of the Royal Society, with Thomas Pennant, a famous zoologist, and with Thomas Jefferson, after whom he named a plant another botanist had discovered. He nourished large dreams, promising over the years a natural history of Pennsylvania, a study of the flora of Virginia, an account of the elements of zoology. He delivered on none of these promises. Most of what he published was trivial, "almost nothing but incomplete tracts, whose faultiness their very title of 'fragments,' 'collections,' and the like sufficiently indicate." He was not above plagarism, and at least twice passed off as his own botanical discoveries made by others. Supposedly he had earned an M.D. at Edinburgh, but the fact was he had left there under a cloud, without his degree and owing money; when this leaked out he tried to buy a degree from a German university. Finally, he was "one of the most irritable and passionate of men." Yet in the flesh he must have seemed abler and more likeable than the record indicates, for he fooled Jefferson.

And he fooled Clark, too, who took charge of getting the journals published after Lewis' death. Barton agreed again to edit the "scientific part" and said he could "do his part in a very short time." Clark said all the dried specimens collected on the expedition will be placed "in your hands" and that Bernard McMahon had been told "to supply you with living specimens when he may have two or more—and to give you every opportunity of inspecting them in his garden, etc." Also, "I have wrote to Mr. Peale requesting him to permit you to describe all and every of the animals, etc., which he has received from the late Lewis and myself." Finally, he was sending George Shannon to Philadelphia to help Barton any way he could. Two years passed with only silence from Barton. Jefferson, ever protective of Lewis' fame, began to fret. He feared that John Bradbury, an English botanist then in the West, was collecting "a great mass of information, which will immediately pass the Atlantic to appear first there." (As it did. Bradbury's *Travels in the interior of America, in the years 1809, 1810, and 1811* was published in London in 1817.) "With respect, therefore, to your work, as well as Governor Lewis'," Jefferson wrote Barton, "I am anxious that whatever you do, should be done quickly." A

year and a half later Jefferson felt the need to send another prod-
ding letter: "When shall we have your book on American botany,
and when the first volume of Lewis and Clark's travels? Both of
these works are of general expectation, and great interest, and to
no one of more than myself."

In 1814 a two-volume narrative of the Lewis and Clark expedition drawn from the journals by Nicholas Biddle was published
in Philadelphia. The following year Dr. Barton died, "without
having I believe done anything towards his share." Seventy-eight
years later Elliott Coues, who edited the Biddle volumes in a way
to emphasize the scientific achievements of the expedition, gave
Dr. Barton the epitaph he deserved. The failure to deliver on his
promise "is the simple explanation of the meagerness of the history
in scientific matters with which the [journals] are replete—to the
keenest regret of all naturalists, and the great loss of credit which
was justly due these foremost explorers of a country whose almost
every animal and plant was then unknown to science." Barton
disgraced himself and his profession by his dereliction, "for in the
meantime others have carried off the honors that belong by right
to Lewis and Clark."

Bibliographical Note

This, as the title says, is a note and will be brief. It is not meant for the scholar, who knows where to go for a full bibliography of the Voyage of Discovery. It is for the layman, whose interest has been aroused and wants to know more about what he has just read.

Start, then, with *Lewis and Clark* (1975), volume 13, in the National Park Service's series on historic sites and buildings. The first half of the book is a detailed and accurate account of the expedition; the second, a long essay on landmarks along the explorers' route as they exist today. The book is profusely illustrated, the maps are superb, the list of "Further Reading," with judicious comments, is hard to improve on, and the price is more than reasonable. (My copy cost $8.35, stock number 024–00500559–5, from the Superintendent of Documents, U.S. Govt. Printing Office, Washington, D.C., 20402.) The only other secondary account I recommend is that of Bernard DeVoto's in the latter half of *The*

Course of Empire (1952). Scholars rarely list DeVoto in their bibliographies, and yet his perceptive summary of the Lewis and Clark Expedition is unquestionably the liveliest and most effective ever written. He knew the land through which they coursed and described it better than anyone before or since.

If, after reading these volumes, the appetite for more lingers, then move on to DeVoto's excellent *The Journals of Lewis and Clark* (1953), a condensation of Reuben Gold Thwaites, *Original Journals of the Lewis and Clark Expedition* . . . (8 vols., 1904–1905, still in print). These were the principal source of the book you have just read. Other editions of the journals—principally Nicholas Biddle's *History of the Expedition* . . . (2 vols., 1814) and Elliott Coues' heavily and marvelously annotated version of the same (3 vols., 1893)—were also used, but Thwaites' was the source finally relied upon. The reader can find other valuable source material listed in the Park Service's volume under "Further Reading," but the only one necessary to mention here is Donald Jackson's *Letters of the Lewis and Clark Expedition, with Related Documents, 1783–1854* (1962; new, enlarged edition 1979). Paul Russell Cutright in his *A History of the Lewis and Clark Journals* (1976), notes what all scholars have long known—that Jackson's collection of documents was the first major contribution to further an understanding of the expedition in over a half century. The second such contribution came two years after Jackson's volume with Ernest S. Osgood's edition of *The Field Notes of Captain William Clark, 1803–1805* (1964).

The difficulty of constructing a bibliography of the Voyage of Discovery is that most readers become fascinated with an aspect of it. Some want to know more, for example, about the flora and fauna discovered. By all means, those readers should go to Paul Russell Cutright's *Lewis and Clark: Pioneering Naturalists* (1969). The title is misleading. Cutright gives an excellent narrative of the entire expedition, and along the way talks about the captains as physicians, ethnologists, geographers, as well as botanists and zoologists. His work has supplemented Elliott Coues' edition of Biddle and is, so I think, the single most valuable secondary book on the expedition.

I have in this book skated blithely past controversies that have kept specialists in the Voyage of Discovery busy and agitated for over a century. Sacagawea, for instance. Was she really important to its success? Thousands of pages have been written seeking to answer that question. See the extensive bibliographies in the books listed above. Did Lewis kill himself? Dawson A. Phelps', "The Tragic Death of Meriwether Lewis," *William and Mary Quarterly*, vol. 13 (1956), pp. 305–18, answered that question for me years ago, but doubters should follow up the material he gives in his ample footnotes.

A few of the best books on specialized aspects of the expedition should be mentioned. On the accoutrements carried by the party see Carl P. Russell, *Firearms, Traps, & Tools of the Mountain Men* (1967). On the land below Fort Mandan see Walter Prescott Webb, *The Great Plains* (1931) and Josiah Gregg, *Commerce of the Prairies* (2 vols., 1844). On Jefferson and the Louisiana Purchase, Alexander De Conde, *This Affair of Louisiana* (1976). On Clark's cartography, John Logan Allen, *Passage Through the Garden: Lewis and Clark and the Image of the American Northwest* (1975). On Charles Willson Peale, the fine biography by Charles Coleman Sellers (2 vols., 1947). On the western Indians there are innumerable books, but I especially recommend Alvin M. Josephy, Jr., *The Nez Perce Indians and the Opening of the Northwest* (1965).

Enough. I could go on and on, but I think the reader has enough to get started. If more is desired, take out a subscription to *We Proceeded On*, an excellent newsletter identified by its publishers as "the official publication of the Lewis & Clark Trail Heritage Foundation, Inc."

Index